To Myra Roberts

Flapjacks & Pot Likker

A Deep Breath of Life

Lossie Rainbolt

Lossie Rainbolt

authorHOUSE®

AuthorHouse™
1663 Liberty Drive, Suite 200
Bloomington, IN 47403
www.authorhouse.com
Phone: 1-800-839-8640

© 2008 Lossie Rainbolt. All rights reserved.

No part of this book may be reproduced, stored in a retrieval system, or transmitted by any means without the written permission of the author.

First published by AuthorHouse 4/30/2008

ISBN: 978-1-4343-6810-2 (sc)

Library of Congress Control Number: 2008903479

Printed in the United States of America
Bloomington, Indiana

This book is printed on acid-free paper.

Acknowledgements

My sincere thanks and love to family and friends who have furnished me with inspiration to tell our story. Thanks to LeVoy Webb, Olene Wright, Neville Saylor, some of my SEARK students and others who have given constructive criticism and helped me edit the manuscript. Special recognition goes to Sandra (Harrington) Green who assisted with her artistic eye in selecting and enhancing photos.

Table of Contents

Chapter 1	A Day with Mom	1
Chapter 2	The Way It Was	6
Chapter 3	School Daze	25
Chapter 4	A Look Around	34
Chapter 5	Texas Saga	39
Chapter 6	Home Again to Belfast	56
Chapter 7	Back to School	70
Chapter 8	High School	88
Chapter 9	Changing Times	95
Chapter 10	Life's Blooming	124
Chapter 11	Cotton-picking Venture	135
Chapter 12	Back to Sheridan and Family Fun	138
Chapter 13	Sawmilling- A Family Venture	144
Chapter 14	Spiritual and Economical Change	151
Chapter 15	An After-school Job, School Honors, and Interrupted Plans	159
Chapter 16	A Miracle Child	161
Chapter 17	First Teaching Jobs	168
Chapter 18	Teaching at Sheridan High School	178
Chapter 19	Decisions and Adjustments	197
Chapter 20	Back to the Present	203

CHAPTER 1

A Day with Mom

We rounded the curve which officially began our tour of Belfast, my mother's old home town in central Arkansas. Nothing much was left now except my mother's memories which she wanted to preserve for me, her oldest son, my younger brother, and her grandchildren. As a child, I had been here many times before, but never viewed the place as anywhere in particular. My dad and mother had bought the old home place from her Dad in 1970. It had fourteen acres of overgrown field covered with thirty-six rusty old car bodies, heaps of old tires, bicycle frames, and piles of tin cans and refuse that people from miles around had dumped. The roof of the front porch on the old house grandfather had built (mainly from four by four timbers and scrap lumber left by a pipe coating company in the field after they had rented it) had caved in and the surrounding yard was covered with wild honeysuckle and berry brambles. Just inside the front room, the roof cap for the stove dangled down leaving a gaping hole with the evening sun pouring through exposing a rotting floor. Dad had taken such pride in cleaning the place up. He and friends hauled off 12 truck and trailer loads of accumulated junk. Dad's friend, Al Smith, had a dump truck which they used to haul the car bodies to a recycle place in Benton. It was interesting to see how they loaded the old cars. Dad had a block and tackle that he used to hoist the cars up into a big oak tree. They backed the dump truck under the swinging car then released it with a bang. A second car body was hoisted up and released on top of the first one. By lifting and banging them together, they smashed the car bodies so they could load three at a time on the dump bed. (I never could figure out how Dad had used the crude tools he had to release the cars at just the right time to have them fall on the right spot.) The recycle place paid $3 each for them, and Dad matched that to give Al expense money for hauling them.

After hauling away the debris, Dad used an old Oliver tractor with a turning plow to plow the land deep. He then ran the disc over it to smooth the clods and planted a crop. I was eleven then and Dad was determined to teach me his work ethic. That old place was transformed into a living vegetable garden with acres of yellow corn, purple beans, tomatoes, okra, sweet potatoes, watermelons, cantaloupes, peas, and peanuts. Dad also decided to have a pond dug in the southwest corner to raise fish and irrigate crops when necessary. We called this small farm "Green Acres" because it reminded us of the TV show by that name. The whole thing turned out to be an overwhelming project. Like a lot of ventures people try, this one turned out to be time consuming and expensive. We spent every moment of spare time at the farm but enjoyed having our own family project. Dad had the expertise to grow the crop, but he lacked the business know-how to market it when it was ready. He finally put an ad in the paper for people to come and pick their own. That was a novel idea then, and some people who had never had the picking experience came from as far away as Little Rock to get fresh vegetables.

Later, Dad tore down the old house because it leaked so badly that it didn't even make a proper barn. During my senior year of high school, he and Mom bought a used mobile home and set it up on the exact spot where great Grandmother Pierce's house once stood. Mom papered the bedroom, and Dad completely renovated the bathroom. They installed new tile and carpet. Some friends and I decided to retrieve the commode that Dad had thrown on a refuse pile. We scrubbed it spotless then painted it metallic blue and gold, our school colors. It was shiny and beautiful. We spent the better part of a night lugging that thing to the roof of the high school, then went home innocently to watch what happened at school the next day when the commode would be discovered. The next morning, students stood near the front of the school laughing and pointing. We joined in the hilarity so as not to arouse suspicion and made our way to class. About mid morning the principal called my friends and me to the office. He had figured out who perpetrated the "crime" and told us to take down our trophy. We good naturedly consented after a few mild protests and heaved our way to the top of the school again to take it down. Just as we got it back on the ground, our English teacher, Mrs. Stuckey said she wanted it for a novel flower container for her back yard. We gladly delivered it, and it stood as a monument of our senior mischief for years to come.

We cleaned out the dug well on the place. It had no culvert but was just a dug hole sixteen feet deep with a board encasement at the top and a roof-like cover. It was hard to believe that a well that shallow could have supplied enough water for a family to live. Mom said the well must have been on a water vein or spring because it had never gone dry during the worst droughts. The water was cool, pure, and tasted good, unlike most other wells around that had "hard" water. People for miles around had hauled water in barrels from the well when their own wells went dry. Dad managed to get some thirty-six inch concrete culverts to put in the well to keep it from caving in on itself and to protect the water from frogs, snakes, and mosquito larvae. Mom said with a little twinkle in her eye that nobody worried about that kind of thing when she was a child.

Dad's health soon failed, and the farm was again somewhat neglected. Mom rented out the field to a neighbor who cut the hay and kept the field from going back to the wild. I grew up and joined the navy. Time passed. Thinking it might one day benefit the family, Mom and Dad kept the old place. The trailer on the farm provided a nice retreat to several of us from time to time. I lived there myself for several years and planted trees and flowers. In 1984, I traded the old mobile home for a new one to put on the same spot. Since I have moved to Little Rock, Mom and I get together on Saturdays and mow the yard. I left a trusty old dog, Rufus, there to guard the place, and I go down twice a week to feed and water him.

It was on one of these occasions that Mom and I were together that she filled me in on some of the history of Belfast as she knew it. As she related her story to me, I looked around and saw the place as a beehive of energy and excitement in days past. I could visualize her as a little girl going through her own struggle to grow up to be a productive person. With a twinkle in her eye, she began her story at her beginning.

CHAPTER 2

The Way It Was

"*Your Grandpa, Jim, contended that the stork* had accidentally dropped me on the way to make a delivery somewhere. He was very mysterious about the whole incident, but said he found me almost naked and crying in a stump hole. Gosh, if I had not been so lucky, I might have been a feral child raised by animals or eaten alive as the case might have been. I always wondered where the stork had really been headed when the accident occurred. Anyway, according to Dad, he took me home, and Mom washed me up and fed me. He said I didn't look like much, but they decided to keep me to see if I might improve. As I grew, I became a grotesque, ever-changing reflection in my own House of Mirrors. It was as though I had stepped through a looking glass, fallen down a rabbit hole, and met the Mad Hatter.

Mine was a topsy-turvy family. The stresses of child birth and economic need caused Mother to become deranged, and

Dad was an illiterate farm and timber worker. My multiple siblings were quarrelsome and mentally challenged. I struggled to figure out where I fit in, to make sense out of senselessness, and to define normal behavior. What great cosmos plan had sent me on this mission? Anyway, here I was!"

Her voice became less playful as she continued: In 1933 Belfast, Arkansas was a booming little timber town. It superseded its sister town by the same name that had been located a few miles northwest near the Tull Community. Old Belfast was a stage coach stop and settlement, while most of the activity of new Belfast centered about the Missouri Pacific Railroad that ran north and south from Benton to Pine Bluff. A crossroad bisecting the railroad led to Palestine community two miles west and the Corinth community on the east. Belfast was originally laid out in lots but soon sprawled in all directions from the focal point of the track and switching spur.

I was born September 11, 1933 to the James Charles Pierce family of Belfast, Arkansas. It was three years after the stock market crash on Wall Street and the middle of the Great Depression (which never ended at our house). My brother took an instant dislike to me because I was "just another girl": the seventh daughter of the seventh daughter (Mom had been the seventh daughter in her family.) Poor Sonny Boy! No wonder he was disgusted! Surrounded by females! Dad believed that this ordinal number gave me some mystical powers that would be a blessing to the family. Life had been so hard for Dad and Mom that whatever hope they could muster to raise their spirits a little was worth something. Crops had failed, mortgage was foreclosed on the home; timber work was scarce; three of seven children had already deceased; the flu epidemic was raging and was to claim Dad's mother and sister Fanny in just a few months. Here was another mouth to feed! There was never enough money for necessities.

Mother despaired of it all and her behavior became so erratic that she was entirely lost in a mental maze. She was taken to the State Hospital for the mentally insane for treatment. Dad loved her so completely. He kept us kids together for three months until she got "better" and came home. Grandma Tribble helped with my care, but she and Dad were never friends. It seems she blamed him for Mom's condition (why didn't he just keep that thing in his pants?) Little was known about postpartum depression and even less about how to treat it. Mom got better and came home. She told us scary, disgusting tales of having to eat bugs and worms. She said she had been to the Bug House. She laughed a hollow laugh, then withdrew into herself and muttered constantly about a straitjacket and electric shock. Dad had scrounged for something to feed me after Mom left. He bought Pet Milk when he could, but I flourished mostly on turnip green pot likker and thickening gravy.

In about a year, my little sister, Betty Jean, was born. Mom's thoughts seemed to grow dark again and she often lost sight of reality, so she had to go away a second time. Betty Jean was a beautiful baby with blue eyes and ringlet curls. She cried a lot with Mom's wonderful, juicy breasts gone. She soon got sick probably from malnutrition. Putrid sores came up all over her little body and she grew worse and worse. Martha, my oldest sister, still a child herself despite her "advanced" age of almost thirteen, wearied of caring for her. Sonny Boy had softened a little toward her when she got sick. She toddled around after him and called him "Bubba" in a small, pleading little voice with arms uplifted to him. One morning he picked her up and held her close as she died in his arms.

Dad arranged for Mr. Trout, the blacksmith, to build a little pine box for Betty Jean's coffin. The neighbors came and lined it with goose feather pillows and satin cloth. They dressed Betty Jean in the loveliest little smocked dress I had ever seen. The collar was embroidered with tiny flowers and had tatted lace around it.

I stood on the foot of the iron bedstead and tried to peek over into the box. When I saw the dress, it took my breath away. I was seized with a momentary tinge of jealously that I did not have anything nearly so fine. Why, I wondered, did she not wake up? What caused the stiff look of her skin? Everyone said not to bother her.

Dad was persuaded against his better judgment to bring Mom home for the funeral. Mom came home that day. I forgot about Betty Jean in my joy to see her. But she only cried, tore at her hair, and plucked at ravelings on her clothes. She argued that her baby was not dead. She would pick me up and lovingly pat me so hard that I had blisters on my behind. Her grip was vise-like and I would be frightened and squirm to get free. She kept trying to feed me milk from her breasts that had dried up months before. I slipped outside and walked around. I found a little wild flower beside the road. I would take that to my mother and she would not cry any more.

Mom looked up briefly when I extended my hand with the flower. She smiled and said it was a sweet william. She knew about flowers from her mother who always had a yard full of them. Her brief smile was fleeting, however, and she quickly retreated back into herself. I tried to put my arms around her, but she pulled away.

Sonny Boy took me by the hand and said, "Sis, I got something to show you." I knew nothing else to do but follow him obediently. What a great surprise! Peanut, our small female dog had puppies in the shed. While I tried to pry the puppies' eyes open, Sonny, somewhat teary eyed, explained to me that Betty Jean was dead, and they were going to put her and the little box into the ground. I would not believe him. "Why do you say that? Nobody would build a box that pretty just to dump in a hole in the ground! You must be goofy!" His further efforts at explanation only confused me, and I grew angry. He said I was a "dumb three-year-old; just a baby." I hit him. We turned again to the puppies as they snuggled against their mother's body nuzzling for warm milk.

When we returned to the house, the box was gone. The aroma of delicious food led us to the kitchen. I had never seen such an array. My Aunt Mary Tribble put her arm gently around me and explained that Betty Jean had gone to visit God, and I assumed she would be back in a few days.

Later, amid the hustle and bustle that followed, I wondered if it were really true that they would actually bury Betty Jean in the ground. Then I remembered the three other little graves in the cemetery where we seemed to be headed. These girls came into the family before I was born. My heart froze with horror and confusion, but nothing arrested the purposeful movement of the procession.

Mother must have sobbed most of the night after the funeral. The next morning with swollen face, wild red eyes, and rumpled hair, she was strangely quiet as though mentally plotting some secret deed. I woke early. Glad that Momma was "better." Daddy was getting off to work. Martha, Mary and Sonny Boy were getting ready for school. Lizzie pretended to feel bad so she could stay home with Mom and me. Momma's spirits seemed to be lifting. She sang a few stanzas of "Old Time Religion." (Maybe, just maybe she would be OK and could stay home with us.) She even made biscuits, cooked eggs and fried potatoes for breakfast.

As soon as everyone left, Momma began doing the dishes. She then started brooding and crying. She ran out the back door with her arms covered with soap bubbles, flopped down face first on the ground and started pulling blades of grass and cramming them into her mouth. By this time she was alternately cursing and crying to high heaven. Then she grabbed Lizzie and me and told us the horrible story. They had buried our sister alive. We had to hurry to the cemetery this morning and dig her up. Momma looked so strangely intent that Lizzie and I were convinced. Yes, we must go and help her right away! Poor little Betty Jean!

Momma gathered a few tools and we started the two-mile walk to the cemetery. The gravels on the road hurt my bare feet. My toes were getting sore, but I didn't want to cause a delay in such an important mission. I tried going faster. My short legs would not work fast enough to keep up with Mamma's hurried, frantic stride. More than once she grabbed me by one arm and hoisted me along with the tips of my toes touching so lightly that I looked like I was doing a funny dance. She dropped the shovel, rake, and hoe and got really mad. She spatted my seat, and I tearfully promised to try harder.

Lizzie was hurrying me, too. She was almost five years older than me. She urged me not to make Momma feel worse. I hadn't thought of making Momma feel bad. Now I felt really guilty. I not only was not hurrying to the graveyard fast enough to rescue my baby sister, but now I was also making Momma feel bad. I was undecided whether this mission was an effort to rescue my little sister or to ease my Momma's feelings.

We slipped quietly past the few houses dotting the gravel roadside. At the last house before we rounded the bend to the Jones Cemetery, I thought I saw a shadow at a window but guessed it was only the wind blowing a curtain.

As soon as we reached the graveyard, I could see a big mound of fresh dirt beside the other three little graves. Momma must be right! We started to dig feverishly, time being of utmost importance. Dirt got in my eyes and hurt. The sun was getting hot. I was thirsty. The hole seemed so deep. Momma said we must hurry. She dug like a dirt moving dragline and scolded us for not digging faster. We were trying, but almost despaired.

Soon we heard a horse coming up the road. Surely whoever it was would help us! It was Mr. John Cranford from the house up the road where I had seen a curtain move when we passed. He said some nasty things to Momma like "Belle you fill that grave back up and come with me. You and these kids don't have any business out here." Momma told him to please don't try to stop us or she would hit him with her shovel. I made ready to help her with a big stick and some dirt clods. Lizzie raised her hoe to threaten him. He got back on his horse muttering something about getting the sheriff.

As soon as he left, Momma gathered the tools, and we started leaving through the woods. I didn't want to leave, but she insisted. It sure bothered me to let that "cranky old man" keep us from getting our little sister out of that hole. Many neighbors began appearing to us in the woods, and Momma was soon smiling and happy as they walked us home. Now I was mad at Momma for not insisting on completing our mission. What about Betty Jean?

That night Daddy was talking kindly loud to Momma. He said something about having to trust her to stay home while he worked and not causing a community uproar. I wondered what a community uproar was then drifted off to sleep again.

Next morning the sheriff came to our house. Momma hid up in the attic. She had a shotgun! She said she would kill Daddy and the sheriff. Soon the sheriff talked her into coming down. They three got into the sheriff's car and drove away. I knew they were taking her back. Helplessly, I stood in the doorway and cried for my Momma.

After that, we children became obsessed with the dead. We made a little cemetery near a spreading sweet gum tree and buried every little dead animal we came across. Once we actually took a dead bird from a cat's mouth, wrapped it in a page torn from the Sears Roebuck Catalog, placed it gently in a match box, and improvised a funeral for the poor thing. We buried it in our cemetery with a lot of fanfare. Waving his arms and pounding a book, Sonny preached a little sermon about heaven while quoting and/or misquoting Bible verses he had heard in church. We girls sang familiar church songs, and we all joined in for proper wailing and mourning before putting the box in the ground and covering it with dirt and colorful glass shards. We were often appalled when we returned later to find dogs and cats had desecrated our precious cemetery and eaten some of our cadavers.

Mom was gone longer this time. Dad would hire Mr. John Smirls to take us to see her about once a month in his pickup truck. We didn't own a vehicle, so it was a special thrill to get to ride in the truck. We knew nothing about seat belts, but could hang on really tight. I loved the feel of the wind blowing through my hair as I viewed the lovely sights along the highway. Mr. Smirls would drive up Arch Street Pike through the East End Community, and I would watch for Mary Lake Castle (at least I thought it was a castle), which was an expansive stone mansion with a lake almost surrounding it. We had heard a lot of strange tales about that house, but it represented fairyland to me. I almost expected to see Cinderella and her Prince Charming walking on the plush, green lawn. Another more modest house a little farther up the road on the right hand side had two huge white bear statues in the yard. I was fascinated by those and hoped another vehicle would not come up or down the road until we passed that house. When a car passed it always stirred up such a cloud of dust that we could hardly see anything for several minutes. Arch Street was still gravel out that far.

When we arrived at the white-washed buildings where they were keeping Mother, we stopped by the office to get permission to see her. All the buildings were locked and only the personnel had keys. As Dad went in to talk to the people in the office, some of the milder patients who were allowed to sit outside approached the truck where we were. They begged for snuff, cigarettes, and candy. An officer attendant came over and shooed them away. Dad soon came out and told us we were to follow the nurse attendant to the building where Mom was. She unlocked the outside door and let us in. There was a long hallway with people sitting on the floor in all kinds of positions.

We were led to a room that was about 8 by 10 feet where we were to wait for them to bring Mom out to see us. The nurse went out locking the door behind her. Then I noticed the bars around the room. We were in a cage! Patients came up and peered curiously at us, and we just as curiously looked at them. I climbed up in Daddy's lap where I felt safe. Soon two nurses came out with Mom in tow. She was not doing well today. All us kids tried to give her a cherry hello. She took one glance at me and commented on how awful I looked. My long stringy hair was matted and my face was dirty. Dad explained that the road dust had settled on all of us, and I had not brushed it off very well. He would see that I got a bath when we returned home.

Mom would not listen. She would not even sit down and talk until she persuaded the nurse to let her give me a bath. The nurse finally agreed to let her take me back to the bathroom. Mom took my hand and led me out. As we started down the hall, one of the patients said, "Oh, there is my baby; my little girl." She grabbed onto me. Mom told her I was not her baby, so the two of them got in a scuffle. I was the rope in a tug of war.

The nurse called another attendant for help and they finally extricated me from all the clutches. As the nurse tried to calm the other woman, Mom grabbed me up and ran to the bathroom with me. She threw me over into the claw foot tub and turned on the hot water. If I hadn't still had my clothes on, I would have been burned badly. I screamed and screamed as the steam boiled up. The nurse came running and rescued me from the tub. She wrapped a big white towel around me and took me back herself where my Dad and the others were waiting. I was a worse mess than ever, and my clothes and hair were wet. Mom came back railing and bitching and refused to calm down and visit. Finally we left. We kids were upset, but Dad told us to think nothing of it that Mom could not help her condition. I was not so sure about her condition, but at that moment, I never wanted to go back to that place again.

In about six months Mom came home again. At first she had some better days. She cleaned the house with feverish energy throwing things mostly out the back door. Once when I was trying to help her, I threw a heavy porcelain door knob out as she was coming back into the house. It caught her smack on the forehead and instantly made a goose egg on that spot. I panicked, horrified at having hurt my mother. She sat down on the ground and put her head in her hands.

Life was almost normal now. Mom was home. We made a garden, had chickens and pigs. There was more to eat. The government set up canning kitchens and taught families how to can food in tin cans. They even had some community workshops on how to make mattresses. Dad worked for the WPA (Work Projects Administration) and helped to build gravel roads where there had been only dirt roads and trails. They moved dirt with road slips pulled by horses. We kids picked blackberries for Mom to can and make cobblers and jelly. Mom joined the Extension Club, a club sponsored by the government to teach women skills that would help them become better homemakers. I got to attend club meetings with her. She had a sociable personality and seemed to be well-liked by the other ladies. They met in each other's homes taking turns being hostess. The hostess always received a nice gift from the group. At one meeting, Mom got a pink depression-glass sugar bowl with a cover. She was so proud of that, but since it was such delicate glass, she was always afraid one of us kids would accidentally break it. I got into big trouble once when I slipped into the kitchen, gently lifted the lid of that bowl and rolled my bubble gum in the sugar. Believe me that did not happen again.

Another incident that probably indicated that I was headed for a life of crime was when I stole an egg from the hen house. I had learned that eggs could be exchanged at Busick's Store for one cent each or traded for merchandise. Since I loved bubble gum so much, I decided I would surreptitiously obtain an egg from the hen house and slip quietly off to the store about a hundred fifty yards from our house and exchange the egg for a piece of bubble gum. It never occurred to me that I would be seen chewing it. Mom caught me and asked me where I got the gum. I lied that I had got it off the bed post where we kids often posted our gum for safe keeping until we wanted to chew it again. Never mind that the flies would blow it. Mom gave me five hard licks. The first two for stealing, the second two for lying, and the fifth one was for a promise of what would happen if I should ever stoop so low again.

Martha, Sonny Boy, Mary, and Lizzie walked to Palestine School some two miles from where we lived. Martha and Sonny Boy could not talk plain. She called me "Offie" instead of Lossie. Lizzie was "Iddie. She said "egg" instead of leg. Those consonant sounds gave her fits and made it hard for people to understand her. Sonny Boy could not learn to read. He fought every day with the kids at school. He always had a victim complex and thought people were making fun of him. Mary could speak, but her writing looked like Chinese characters. Lizzie progressed well with reading, but was as quarrelsome as a ferret, and couldn't get along with anyone. The teacher spanked her two or three times every day. She always yelled to high heaven and circled round and round the teacher as the action went forward. She talked baby talk so we started calling her Snooks from the radio character Baby Snooks.

For some mysterious reason, Lizzie was beginning to get a hump in her right shoulder. It seemed that the left shoulder quit growing normally and the right shoulder grew up in a hump. She had a long spell of high fever when she was about five. Everyone thought she had completely recovered but later the growth patterns took an odd turn.

It seemed I was always an accident waiting to happen. I bumped against a red hot heater one winter just as I was toddling, and burned my left knee cap badly. Later that year in late spring Mother was outside washing beets to can. I woke up late and went in to the table to find something to eat. I got a meat fork and was going to spear a piece of cold fried meat when a fly buzzed around my face. I hit at it with the fork and stuck myself in the right eye. It got infected and matted constantly. For almost two years, it bothered me. Finally I could hardly see out of either eye. The infection had spread along the optic nerve. Dr. O.R. Kelly came by our house to see about Mother and saw me. He said I must have an operation right away.

Mother, who was pregnant again, went ballistic What if I didn't wake up when they put me to sleep? She brought up so many "what ifs" in her tearful state, that I contracted her fear and thought I was going to die, too. The older kids weren't any help with their talk of people dying on the operating table.

One thing was to save me from the awful death-defying operation. Dad had no money to pay for it. I was somewhat relieved, but that was short-lived. Dad confided to Dr. Kelly about our financial situation and he asked Dad about mortgaging our house to pay for it. Dad agreed and had the papers drawn. Dr. and Mrs. Kelly came for me early one morning. (The doctor refused to accept the mortgage, but said he was just testing to see how willing my dad would be to do his part.) I saw their car coming up the dirt road to our house, and I felt my heart thumping hard against my chest. Where could I hide so no one would find me? Then I thought of the out door toilet. No one would look in that smelly place. I shot out the back door and made a bee line to the toilet.

I hunkered down in the tightest little ball I could squeeze into. The stench was gagging, but I would have endured anything to keep this from happening. Everybody was calling my name and looking for me. I prayed they would not find me. Then Martha and Mary thought of the out-house. They dragged me out like two hunters who had bagged their prey. I hated their smug smiles and was satisfied only by thinking of how they were going to moan and groan when I was dead.

Mrs. Kelly was such a nice lady. She hugged me and assured me that everything would be ok. They took me to their car which was the most magnificent vehicle I had ever seen. It had plush seats with all kinds of knobs and gadgets. Mrs. Kelly kept talking to me about other things. Did I like paper dolls? I told her how Lizzie and I loved to play paper dolls. We cut people out of the Sears Roebuck Catalog and made whole families. We used empty match boxes for our cars and shoe boxes for our houses. Sometimes we had to rescue the catalog from the outhouse because it was commonly used for toilet paper.

"Well," she said kindly, "when you come back home, I will buy you a real paper doll book with punch out dolls and clothes." That was a promise that gave me courage. No other kid I knew had a real paper doll book like that. I had seen them in stores a few times when I had got to ride the train to Sheridan, but never dreamed of really owning one.

By the time we arrived at Arkansas Childrens Hospital in Little Rock, I had ceased to dread the ordeal ahead of me. Inside the hospital, the nurses washed me and prepped me for surgery. They put this funny little robe on me that was split all the way down the back and kept balling up around me when I lay down.. I liked their smiles and tenderness, something I was not accustomed to receiving. They put me in a small bed with railings on it. It smelled so fresh and clean with real white sheets. Surely these nice people would not let harm come to me.

Just as I was so reassured, they put a sort of mask lightly over my face and told me to take a deep breath. Whoa! What was this! They *were* going to put me to sleep! All the syrupy sweetness was just a diversion! I struggled briefly as I felt firm hands holding my arms, legs, and head. I don't know how much later I awoke. My whole head was covered with bandage with holes for nose and mouth. I must have looked like a mummy. I was so sick to my stomach that I threw up all over the bed. People rushed in and cleaned up the mess. Was I in heaven?

I heard someone swear mildly and knew that words like that would not be used in heaven. Hopefully, I was not in the bad place. I soon realized that I was indeed still alive. The attendants insisted that I lie with the right side of my head down. They whispered something about the infection must drain, and asked each other if they thought I might see when the bandages were removed. It seemed like days that my head was bandaged and my neck was stiff from holding my head in the same position.

Finally came the big day! The doctor slowly removed the bandage. It took a bit of coaxing because it was matted with drainage. The lights blinded me as I squinted to see all the nurses anxiously hovering around my bed. The doctor asked me questions about what I could see, and as I named the items around me, the whole room erupted with applause. Little did I realize what a truly great day that was!

It must have been a couple more weeks that I stayed in the hospital. My eye socket was healing and I was fitted with a glass eye. The nurses took me to the kitchen with them, sat me on the counter, and fed me ice cream. Ice cream was a novelty to me. Sometimes the family made homemade ice cream with a crank freezer on the 4th of July. Except for that, we made ice cream from snow using Pet Milk, sugar, and vanilla flavoring in the winter when it came an occasional snow deep enough that was not mixed with sleet. I thrived on all the attention and was curious to look at the eye socket when the glass eye was taken out for cleaning.

Soon it came time to go home. I could hardly wait to show my brother and sisters my new eye. It moved just like the other one, and was not painful at all. Dr. and Mrs. Kelly came to get me. As she had promised, she brought the wonderful paper doll book. They told me I had a new baby sister at home and they would take me by to see her. I was to stay with the Kellys a week or so. They wanted to make sure the new eye did not get infection behind it and cause me problems again.

When we got back to Belfast, my family was waiting, and Mom showed me the new baby. Mom looked shaky and white. She tried to smile, but she talked to herself and was distracted. The older kids were surprised (and I thought a bit envious) to see how the new eye looked. We stayed only a short time then the Kellys took me home with them. Wow! This was the life! They had an indoor toilet, running water, fluffy beds, a proper living room, and French doors separating the living room and formal dining room.

I enjoyed the new arrangement. Mrs. Kelly read stories to me. I remember "The Little Red Hen" as my favorite. I asked her to read it over and over and over. The Kellys also had a black maid that was the first black person I ever remember seeing. She was so black that her teeth looked like pearls when she smiled. She read the story "Little Black Sambo" to me, and I got the impression that black people were very inventive and intelligent. After all, Little Black Sambo outwitted all the tigers and got a big stack of pancakes for his ingenuity.

In a few weeks, the eye healed pretty well. The glass eye matted a lot and my nose got in the way when I tried to look around without turning my head. My range of vision was lessened with only one eye, and I had to adjust to changing depth perception, but mostly I was ready for action. I went home torn between my wish to stay in such a nice place with wonderful people and the desire to be in familiar surroundings with my own family. I was happy to find that the family had named my little sister Ellen in honor of Mrs. Ellen Kelly who had been so good to me. Ellen had no middle name. Just Ellen was enough! It was my family's expression of deep gratitude.

Things changed so fast. Mom was getting worse and worse again. Dad was afraid to leave us kids alone with her while he went to work. Even though she was at nature a loving mother, sometimes she didn't seem aware of other tendencies. She could not take any event in stride, but overreacted to everything. Either she was deliriously happy or sunk in the depths of gloom. She could change in a moment without notice or apparent provocation.

Finally Dad made the hard decision to take her back to the State Insane Asylum. What would we all do now? As shaky as the props of our life had been, they seemed to be cracking under strain. After a few days little Ellen was crying almost constantly. As concerned as we were, we didn't know what to do. When Ellen was three months old, an angel appeared. My Aunt Cora Tribble came over and generously offered to take Ellen and keep her for us. Daddy gave his permission, but would not give her up for adoption.

She got the best of care and love from the Tribbles. It was truly a Godsend. As Ellen grew, Aunt Cora trained her beautiful hair to have fashionable finger curls. She was by far the prettiest girl in the family. Lucky for her, too, when she had pneumonia, they took care of her and she survived. We did not need another little grave in the cemetery.

Back at home, the rest of us tried to rally like scattered troops. Nights were getting longer and gradually colder. The quilt pallet I slept on left a lot to be desired in the way of comfort. Dad worked that problem out by having all four of us girls sleep in the same bed. Martha and Mary at the head and Lizzie and I wedged in at the foot. Sleep was almost impossible with someone's smelly feet always in our faces, feet kicking us, and long toenails scratching. Almost inevitably someone wet the bed most nights and the mattress had to be aired almost every day. If it didn't dry completely, we turned it over or covered it with quilts. When Jimmy Dickens came out years later with the song, "Sleeping at the Foot of the Bed" I could certainly identify with the lyrics. It was much warmer under there if one could endure the smell, but like turtles, we had to come up for air. One night when I was sick, Dad put me in the bed between him and Sonny Boy. I vomited all over them both. Sonny mouthed about that for forty years. Dad just got up and cleaned us all up.

CHAPTER 3

School Daze

*M**om had left the last time in* August. In September, Dad decided that since he had to work, I would have to go to school with the older children even though I was not yet quite 5 years old. Palestine School was a two-storied wooden structure with grades 1-6 on the lower floor and grades 7-8 were upstairs. I had to give my word of honor to sit quietly during class. Can you imagine how hard that was? The teacher was Jewel Doris Gillis just a young girl, I believe she was still in her teens. She taught all six grades in the lower part. I would listen to the older students recite their lessons and would soak up many of the lessons by osmosis through my skin. Jump rope, hop scotch, and jacks were the preferred games for girls during recess. The boys usually played baseball.

    Miss Gillis was so pretty. She had long, dark hair and full lips that were painted with red lipstick. Her smile spread fully across her face and made it light up with enthusiasm. She decided to give me a reader like the first grade students had, so when she called up the first grade to read, I got to go, too. I memorized that book! I wanted her to be proud of me. Once, though, when she called me to read, I eagerly read, "The rooster crows to wake me up. The hen lays eggs for my buttercup." She had not had time to open the book. She was not pleased! She said, "You are not reading. You are reciting." I didn't know what the difference was, but soon found out. To read, I had to look at every word as I said it. She somehow knew that I did not know one word from another. I tried again, and soon was reading as well as the others in my group.

School was my element. I enjoyed being around the other students, and always yearned to know things. Our desks were the old fashioned desks with decorative iron frames that had a seat wide enough to seat two small children in front with a desk built behind it. These were anchored to the floor in neat rows. We had the messy inkwells on the desk that were continually getting tipped and letting ink spill everywhere. Boys loved to get a girl's braid and dip it in the inkwell causing a ruckus that would interrupt class for a few minutes. We took our lunch to school. Mine was usually peanut butter and crackers or a biscuit sandwich of Tip Top meat. The heat gave it a funny smell and it was not very appetizing.

My brother would often snatch my lunch and eat it himself on the way to school. My teacher sometimes found out when I didn't have lunch and would take me to her house near the schoolyard where her mother always had a scrumptious meal prepared. I loved that and secretly hoped Sonny Boy would eat my lunch more often. The lunch I liked best, however, was the noon spread where all the students would spread out whatever they had brought, and we could help ourselves to what we liked best. It was interesting to see what the others brought. I have always compared that to a church fellowship.

Sonny Boy developed an attitude about school. He couldn't read and would try to entertain the class with antics that the teacher could not tolerate. Mr. Green, teacher for the seventh and eighth grade, would pull Sonny's hair instead of spank him. The other kids took to teasing him and pulling his hair also. One day Sonny came home and asked Daddy to cut all his hair off. Daddy didn't understand why, but did it for him. The next morning, Sonny soaked his head with Rose Hair Oil and set off for school smelling good. Later that day when the teacher tried to pull his hair, he got a hand full of oil. Everyone laughed because Sonny made the teacher look foolish. Needless to say, Sonny was not his favorite student after that.

Martha made it to the eighth grade. She learned to do square root in math. She bragged about her superior knowledge all the time, and often said, "Oooh can't eben do squeare oot, en I can." I didn't know what square root was, but it sounded like something really important to know. Some day I thought I would learn to do it just to show her.

Soon the health department stepped in and tried to make our lives intolerable by insisting we get typhoid and diphtheria shots. The older kids painted images of long needles that would poke right through your arm. I hoped there was some way to avoid that ordeal. When the nurses came to school to give the shots, I slipped quietly out the door and headed toward home. As I went, I decided that I had better not go home so early, so I hid in the Belfast Church building. God would protect and comfort me there I thought; however, even God could not be depended on to support my distress because the older kids came to get me. I missed the shots that day, but the nurses came back a week later and I was cornered. I watched a few kids in front of me get theirs and it didn't seem like the big deal I thought it was going to be. I felt a little foolish for being such a "fraidy cat."

A well across the road provided water for the school. Its curb was made of native rock and a shingle roof protected the contents from falling debris. It furnished cool water for travelers on State Highway 35 and the Belfast road. Usually the older boys would draw fresh water about twice a day and bring it over to the school. The teacher had us to each bring our own drinking glass and write our name on it. She said people got germs from drinking from someone else's glass and if one person was sick, many people could get the sickness. I didn't much believe in germs because I couldn't see them, but a lot of people were always getting sick so it was worth a try.

We kids at first did not have a toilet, but had to go down in the woods across from the school until we were properly hidden. A trail to the left was for the girls, and a trail to the right was for the boys. Leaves served as wiping paper. In winter when the trees were bare, it was hard to find a hiding place to make a nature call. If we needed to go to the woods during class, we were to raise one finger for number one business and two fingers for number two. Number two usually got top priority. Once when I raised my hand with one finger up, the teacher ignored me because there were so many clamoring to go. She tried to let girls go at one time and boys at another. I needed to go really bad, but she would not give me permission. Finally when I got permission, I just barely made it across the road and I flooded the ditch. I proceeded somewhat straddle legged down into the woods and gathered leaves to stuff in my panties. When I slipped back into class, those things kept falling out as I walked, and the other kids laughed and laughed at me.

By the spring of 1940, all the children at the school were excited that summer vacation was near. I was especially excited because I was being promoted to third grade. I was now six years old. It was a custom in all school districts to have a closing program. The program involved all students participating in some way, usually in ways that had very little to do with the grind of everyday class work. The Palestine teachers Miss Jewel Doris Gillis (still teaching elementary grades 1-6) and Mr. Joe Johnson (grades 7 and 8) were in charge of this spring extravaganza. Pressure was on! They puzzled over what each student could do to entertain the parental audience that would be sure to pack the house.

My siblings were especially hard to accommodate because they all had speech impediments. Sonny Boy, who was still in seventh grade and in spite of all efforts had not learned to read, was to carry the American flag to center stage and lead everyone in the Pledge of Allegiance. Two girls from the upper class were to then sing "God Bless America."

My sisters, Martha and Mary, agreed to sing together for the next number. They chose a hymn entitled "This World Is Not My Home," a familiar song they had heard many times in church, and one that the audience might recognize in spite of the fact that neither could carry a tune nor harmonize in any way. This was a cacophony that was sure to rock the house. Nevertheless, they practiced at home hours on end screeching out the words, never in unison. Martha was always loudest and rushed ahead in song while Mary was more deliberate. The results were not unlike the rowboat song, and each rendition produced a different flavor and texture.

Probably the best act our family had to offer was Sister Lizzie's. She was always outspoken and show offish. Someone had made her a brilliant blue dress out of crepe paper, and her lovely blue eyes sparkled like sapphires. She looked stunning and aptly represented the historical personage, Betsy Ross. She sat beside a table pretending to sew a flag and recited a poem. A glass of water was on the table along with a kerosene lamp to give an authentic look to the scene, and in one of her sweeping gestures with her sewing arm, she knocked over the water which ran down the paper dress. The crepe paper began to look limp as she stood up and made a blue streak running off stage.

As for me, my role was to appear on stage with three other little girls. We each were to have a doll buggy to push forward and back as we said little rhymes in our turns. What fun, I thought, until I remembered I had no doll buggy. In fact, I had no doll either. I had never owned a doll. The only facsimile I had was a doll my mother had made from a print on a flour sack. It was mostly flat with puffy knots in the wrong places. That doll just simply would not do for an important occasion like this. The carriage was another problem. Never had I even dreamed of having a fancy little doll carriage decorated with eyelet lace and colorful flowing pastel ribbons like the other girls in my group. Wow! What to do?

Fleeting thoughts of how to get out of this situation skittered through my mind. Maybe I could pretend to be sick….no, that was not a good option. Dad would just whip out the Black Draught, castor oil, or 666 and insure my quick recovery by turning my insides wrong side out. I could jump out of a tree and maybe break a leg, but what if I broke my neck instead? I came home, and with hopeless frustration, went outside and flopped down in a chicken hole in the back yard and cried in desperation.

In the meantime, the older children told my dad and some neighbors about my need for a doll and buggy. A neighbor lady offered to loan me one of her little girl's dolls. She hastened to get it and brought it back. That doll simply took my breath away! It was a life-sized infant. It had black hair with ringlet curls, sparkling brown eyes that opened and closed, head, arms and legs of compressed sawdust smoothed to perfection and painted over to look like real skin. The body was stuffed canvas. She was dressed in an infant's dress with smocked, briar-stitched front, and little embroidered animal figures surrounded the hem of the skirt. I took her in my trembling arms while the lady cautioned me to "take good care of her." How could I not take care of her?

My joy over the doll was soon shattered when I realized I still needed a carriage. Any doll this magnificent need the finest. Dad assured me that he would try to find one for me since the program was three or four days away. Meantime, I took the doll to school to practice the routine. I proudly carried my baby on stage and held her gently while the other girls jiggled their buggies back and forth. They unkindly referred to the fact that I was not doing it right because I had no carriage. I told them my dad would get me one before the program. As one day passed, then another, my heart slowly sank. Then the awful doubts began to return. Would my dad really be able to find a carriage that we could borrow? I threw myself into learning my lines and knew everyone's lines by heart. I would quietly prompt the others when they hesitated.

The day of closing night I trudged the two miles home with heavy heart. Dad met me at the door with the widest grin I had ever seen him wear. "I have a surprise for you," he announced proudly. Butterflies started to soar in my chest. Had he found a carriage for me after all? He pointed near the window. The room was dark when I stepped inside, but as my eye adjusted, I could see what looked like a small rocking chair in the dim light. Dad had spent the whole day making it for me from little pieces of wood he found around the house. It was just the right size for my borrowed doll. The rocker parts were whittled from soft pine. The seat was made from heavy cardboard, the sturdy three-layered cardboard with corrugated center. Underneath the seat was the original lettering to the box, PET MILK. This was really some little contraption. It was cute and jaunty looking, but had not a smidgeon of paint. "A crude sight this chair will make beside the fine carriages in the program," I thought. But Daddy was so happy about solving my problem that I couldn't tell him how I really felt.

Reluctantly, I resigned myself to accepting the jeers and snide remarks that were sure to come. I would hold my head up and make the best of this. When we got to school, the little girls rushed to see what I had brought. I put on a good front and showed them my little chair, set the doll in it and demonstrated how it would rock her. One mother remarked that it was certainly "one of a kind." No one else had anything like it. Suddenly, to my total surprise, the atmosphere changed.

The little girls started clamoring that they wanted a little chair like that. They no longer put stock in their store-bought buggies, but thought my little rocker was the grandest thing they had ever seen. And I really thought so, too. My bare toes dug into the floor proudly as I recited my part. We got a standing ovation.

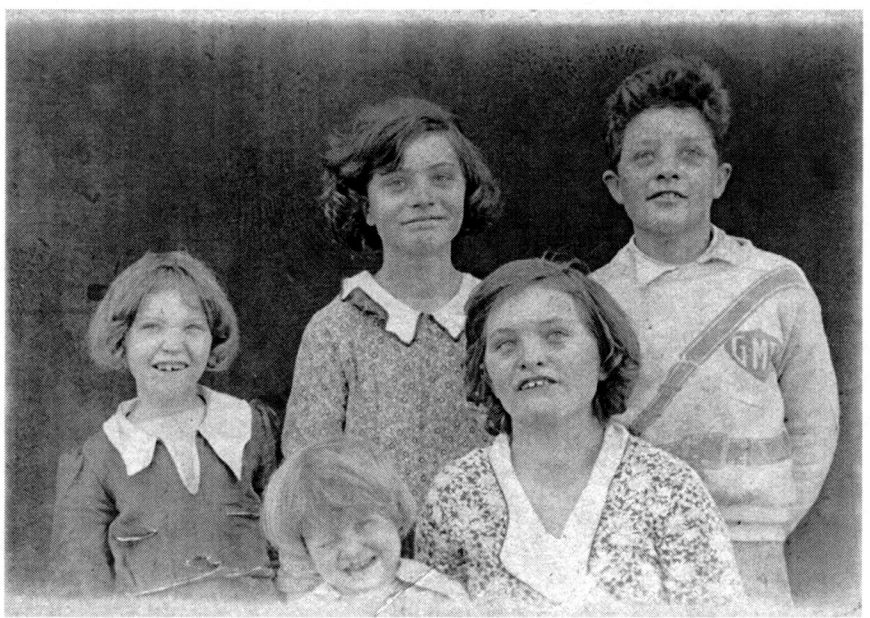

Lossie and Siblings

CHAPTER 4

A Look Around

Summer vacation gave me time to explore and I began to observe the activity around my home. Our house was about 150 yards from Busick's General Mercantile Store, a brick edifice, impressive as the only brick structure in the neighborhood, was located on the corner bordering the road that ran south adjacent to the Missouri Pacific railroad track. The train ran down the tracks from Benton to Pine Bluff early each morning and came back some time in late afternoon. It brought the mail in heavy bags stamped with "U. S. Mail" in large letters. Mr. Busick was the Belfast postmaster and had the post office in the west end of his brick store. He had a big, shaggy dog that looked like the movie dog Bethoven. The dog's name was Bounce. He would always bark and cavort around shaking loose hair and ticks all over the Busick yard when he heard the train coming. Excitement grew in proportion to the clatter and clacking of the train as it blew its whistle for the crossing.

Puffing a huge cloud of smoke, it lumbered like a heavy giant down the track into the center of town. That was the signal for Mr. Busick to make sure the mail bags were in the large mail box out near the tracks. The conductor would collect the bags and put out other bags that contained incoming mail for Belfast residents. The train "switched" for a few minutes picking up flat cars loaded with pulp wood or cross ties and leaving some empty ones to be filled the next day. I often wondered where they were going.

Virginia Harrington, a little girl about my age, lived diagonally across the tracks from my house. In the afternoons, we listened for the train, and the instant we heard Bounce barking, we knew it would soon be in our earshot. We would make a bee line to beat one another to the switch crossing where we knew the train would stop and the conductor would toss us a handful of pennies which landed in the cinders about the track. We got on hands and knees and scrambled to find those pennies. Sometimes we surreptitiously placed pennies on the track for the train to run over. It was funny to see how squished the face on the coin looked after the train had run over the coin. My dad found out and put a stop to the pennies on the track. He said they might cause a train wreck and people would get killed.

One of my favorite pastimes was to stand on the knoll halfway between my house and the store and watch the trucks bring in pulpwood to load on flat rail cars. Usually this was done by strong, young black men. They used a cant hook to get a stick end up in one arm and then hooked the other end with a sweeping motion as they tossed the heavy sticks on the flatcar. Those men would sing and chant in unison. Their strong muscles would ripple rhythmically and torsos glisten with sweat. The whole picture was a living work of art. I was a few hundred feet from where they worked, so we never spoke, but I felt a strange affinity to them as though we all fit into some great scheme of the universe.

The train not only carried the mail and took the timber products to market, but it also provided transportation for Belfast residents. For twenty cents we could catch the train as it came down in the morning, ride the red caboose to Sheridan where we got off, and catch it back home as it came back from Pine Bluff in the afternoon. That would give us three or four hours to tend to business and buy a few things we needed that were not available in Belfast. The Missouri Pacific railroad was the center of life in this community.

Another point of interest in Belfast was Joe Webb's store which was directly across the road from Busick's store. The appearance of this store was in stark contrast to Busick's. While Busick's store was immaculate both inside and out, the Webb place of business was just the opposite. Instead of brick, it had wooden clapboard siding that looked weathered and old. The steps at the side door where the customers entered were littered with cigarette butts, coke lids, candy wrappers, and other carelessly thrown items. Spilled gas soaked the ground and steps near the entrance. The gas pump was operated by a hand lever that pumped the gas up into a glass reservoir at the top to be gravity fed into a vehicle with a nozzle much like modern gas pumps.

A large "feed room" on the left side of the entryway had all kinds of livestock feed. Joe's chickens entered the store freely from his back yard and laid eggs in the feed room.

Sometimes his pigs that roamed free in the back yard with the chickens would lumber up the back steps and pay a brief visit. The several hound dogs he kept slept lazily by the box heater looking up only occasionally when Uncle Joe would give them a wrapper from a slice of bologna.

In spite of his unkempt appearance and lack of sanitation, Uncle Joe (no relation, just a term of respect) probably had more money than anyone else in Belfast and gave credit to the downtrodden more freely than his competition. His was a real jot-em-down store. Records were kept on walls, calendars, paper bags, writing pads, or whatever was handy when a customer came in. When a person went in to pay a bill, Uncle Joe might have to look in five different places to round up all the credit charges. Some suspected that he may have sometimes put a charge on a good paying customer's account to be sure of his return.

As far back as I can remember, Uncle Joe drank heavily and cussed freely, but some of the people said that at one time he was a Christian and had helped establish Belfast Missionary Baptist Church. Life is strange, and you never know what happens inside a person's mind and heart. As a child, I could see through his rough veneer and viewed a kindly man. He never raised his voice, but was always invoking God's help to damn something. When a customer came in, Uncle Joe would just stuff money into his shirt pocket when he was paid for an item, and often the money fell out onto the floor. Most people in Belfast were honest enough to pick it up for him and return it.

Rumor was that much of the Webb money came from operation of illegal stills during prohibition, but no one would testify as much. Dad said Uncle Joe made money on buying up flour and staples before the rationing and then selling them to people in need. One thing I was sure of was that Uncle Joe had a good heart and would never turn down anybody he could help. He had befriended Dad so much through the years until Dad was now heavily in debt (over $1000) to him.

Dad was a man of honor about paying his debts but saw no way out because the need to feed us kids and keep a roof over our heads cost more than he could manage. One can't budget when there is nothing to budget, and work was seasonal. Soon, a glimmer of hope came. The Joe Bryant family had visitors from the Rio Grande Valley of Texas. Some of my cousins, Roy Bryant, his wife Willie, two children Billy and Geneva, and my bachelor cousin Manoline Bryant, came to visit their Dad, Joe Bryant, who lived just across the field from us. Joe Bryant had been married to Dad's sister who died the year I was born. The nephews convinced Dad that there was plenty of work in the Valley. They said "Money grows on trees there." They were referring to the citrus harvest in the fall of the year. He should go there.

CHAPTER 5

Texas Saga

Dad *thought it was worth a try,* so he sold all the chickens and hogs, bought an old model A truck, loaded our few personal belongings along with us five kids, and headed down the road to Texas. We looked like an early caricature of "The Beverly Hillbillies." No one mentioned that the Valley was a thousand miles away and the road was gravel almost all the way. Dad could not drive very well and had no driver's license, but we chugged along. About every ten miles or so, we would have a flat tire. Dad would hop out, jack up the truck, take off the wheel, pull out the tube and put on glued or vulcanized patches. He replaced every thing, then pumped air into the tire again with a hand pump. I was curious about the patches. The vulcanized ones held better than the glued ones. We had a good day if we made a hundred miles.

At night, we found an open area near the road and pitched camp. Martha and Mary were to cook some supper on a portable kerosene heater. The meal was nearly always fried potatoes and flapjacks. They knew little about cooking so the food was in a semi-state of doneness and burnt. We were so hungry we could have eaten the utensils by mealtime. Sonny and Dad cleaned off the ground a little with a garden rake and threw off the mattresses. With a few feed-sack sheets and a quilt or two, we were ready for dreamland. Dew formed on the covers and whatever parts of our bodies were sticking out.

One night when we had camped at a park in Hubbard, Texas, heavy black clouds boiled up on the horizon, the wind came in strong gusts. Dad routed us up from sleep, and we all helped load things in the truck and covered them with canvas. Then he stacked all five of us kids in the cab pushing us together until we fit. He then sat down by a huge spreading oak tree, covered himself with a long heavy coat, and weathered the storm. I could see him out the fluid windshield of the truck cab when the lightning flashed.

Morning came and we kids roused from fitful slumber and extricated ourselves from the truck cab. We were all stiff from being cramped in the same position all night. Dad had shed the protective coat, recovered the kerosene stove from the truck bed, and started some coffee and fried potatoes. Except for the ground being a bit soggy, everything looked fresh and clean. Lizzie and I looked around and saw a couple of girls playing near a large tent. We went over to say "Hi" and were soon playing hopscotch with them. I don't remember their names, but every time we began playing one game, the bigger girl would say, "Wait a minute, wait a minute, let me see." Then she would decide another game to try. She did that so often that it became a personal joke to Lizzie and me. When we were in private, one of us would say "wait a minute, wait a minute, let me see," and we would both giggle hysterically. The girl had an afflicted 10-year-old brother who would take the caps off gas tanks and breathe the fumes. When we cleaned out a place to play house and set up some pretend tables and stools, he would come around and knock everything down. He was the bane of our lives the few weeks we were in the camp. We thought those folks were wealthy because they lived in a nice tent with a floor.

Lizzie and I walked the mile or so to Hubbard one day and a lady who was standing in front of her store was moved with compassion for Lizzie because she had that hump on her back. She called us in and gave Lizzie a brand new dress and some candy. I foolishly wished for a time that I had a hump, too, so someone would give me something.

While we were there at camp my sister Mary got bit by a spider. She had sat down on a pile of clothes that she and Martha were going to wash and the spider was hidden in the clothes. Dad took her to a doctor, and the place on her leg rotted nearly to the bone before it finally healed.

Dad was picking up a bit of farm work. Usually I got to go along and help what I could. I had to be careful when I jumped down off the truck, because sometimes I landed on goat heads. These were stickers that grew on stalks much like Arkansas cockleburs except that the goat heads had longer stickers and were shaped like a goat's head. They would drop off the stalks and scatter about with the wind. I was always barefooted and those things could draw blood. We worked the onion harvest at one time. We pulled the onions and cut the tops off and let them lie on the ground a few hours until the tips were about dry then bagged them in 100 lb. net bags. That was a smelly job, and I had to remember not to rub my eyes even when the onions brought tears.

One day Dad found us a house about three miles from Hubbard. It was really a shotgun shack hidden by tall weeds, but provided a roof over our heads, and there was a swamp nearby that I thought was a nice pond. We moved our few worn belongings into it. Still it was more like camping because we had no bedsteads or furniture, just some old mattresses, the kerosene cook stove, and a few cooking utensils. We ate from bucket lids. Dad made everyone use spoons only. After the incident with my eye, he took no chances on forks. We didn't know even the rudiments of proper manners in anything except we were required to wash face and hands before eating and all sit at the table together and eat at the same time. I assumed that was to give everyone a fair start at the food. We ate buffet style with all the food dishes on the table and passed it around when someone asked for it. It was beans and potatoes one day and potatoes and beans the next.

After we got settled in our home, the landlord hired us to harvest corn. He had fields and fields of corn. Dad tried to get me to drive the two horses with the wagon down the rows. He and the others were to pick the corn and throw it into the wagon. Those horses were not about to mind my squeaky little voice. They would pull every which way. I tried tightening the reins and they reared up, then pranced and danced and tromped down a big area of corn. There was lots of yelling and choice expletives on all sides. I lost my first job as CEO of the cornfield.

Our diet of beans and potatoes began to be a little varied. The farmer gave Dad some of the dried field corn we had been harvesting. We kids scoffed because we didn't see how we could possibly eat that corn, but Dad knew. He filled the wash pot with water and built a fire around it. When the water began to boil, he added some Merry War lye then dumped about a half bushel of shelled corn into the pot. We used the lye to wash clothes, but knew it was poison to eat. This looked risky to me. Dad boiled the corn in the lye water until the tough outside layer of the grains began to peel off. He then dipped the corn out and doused it into cool water. He scrubbed the grains together until the husks were removed and floating to the top. It was a simple matter to separate the tough husks from the corn. Dad rinsed the corn about ten more times, and voila! We had a huge dishpan full of hominy. What a wonderful snack we had for a whole week!

Sonny Boy soon discovered that there were a few fish in the "pond" behind the house, so on Sundays, he would go pole fishing. He tried to discourage me from following him (I still idolized him, but he had never completely forgiven me for being a "girl".) I was so persistent that he soon relented and gave me the job of catching grasshoppers for bait. He would catch a string of sun perch which we cooked very brown and ate bones and all.

As soon as the corn was harvested, there was cotton to pick. Dad tied some straps to a 100 lb. flour sack and I used that for picking cotton. I was to pick enough cotton to fill it every day. That was a breeze. We soon moved on toward the Valley. There was harvest of some kind from early spring to late fall in different areas of Texas. Work was seasonal and workers flocked in by the thousands. The government and farmers were overwhelmed with excess labor force at times but desperate when workers were needed and could not be found. Officials began to look for solutions to the problem. A Federal Security System was soon put in place to direct the migrant workers to the areas where they were needed.

Dad had made friends with a widowed man from Kansas, J.C. Booth, who had two sons Ray and Clyde. The two fathers decided we would all travel together. Mr. Booth was more familiar with Texas territory than Dad was, so he made a good guide. Clyde was seven and Ray was nine. They were really into cowboys so I played shoot-em-up with them from dawn to dusk wherever we stopped our caravan for a time. We had sticks for guns which quickly morphed into horses to get away from the bad guys.

We picked more cotton at another place. Mary found a baby jackrabbit asleep under a cotton stalk. She gave it to me, and I was overjoyed. I put it in my cotton sack with my cotton, but when I emptied the sack on the wagon, I forgot and dumped my rabbit. I didn't think of it until I got back out to the field. Oh, my gosh! I rushed back, climbed up into the cotton wagon, and searched for my rabbit. I found it nestled cozily in the corner. That afternoon when we rode the wagon home, there was an elderly Mexican man riding beside me. He smiled and said, "conejo" and pointed at the rabbit. I did likewise and said, "Rabbit." By the time I got off the wagon the old gentleman and I were exchanging words in Spanish and English and having a great time. I had wondered why the Mexicans picked cotton on one side of the field and we picked on the other side. Every time I got my flour sack filled, I would slip across the cotton field near to where they were working, lie down in the middle, and just listen to the musical sound of their language. They were always laughing and seemed like a happy people.

Finally we reached the Valley. The Booths went to stay a few days with their Uncle Frank who I think lived at McAllen. We stayed a day or two with the Henry Williams family, relatives of the Bryants. Dad looked around and found housing in a migratory labor camp just outside of Weslaco, Texas. We had two rooms made of concrete blocks. The camp was laid out just like a small town with neat rows of adjoining rooms. We lived at the north end, and our rooms faced the community square where there were public bathroom, showers, and a place with tubs and rub boards to do laundry. This was really far better than sleeping under the stars. When we first moved in, we worked the fruit harvest. I found out oranges are not naturally orange, that dye is added to their peel to make them more attractive. I learned to eat grapefruit by slicing it open and digging out the pulp so I would not taste the bitter layer next to the peel. Tangerines were plentiful, too, and I ate so much citrus that my teeth were like razors.

The fruit harvest soon ended, and Dad was out of work again. He could not pay the rent on our rooms. He talked to the superintendent of the camp and they put him to work cleaning the garbage stations. There were about 10 garbage stations at the end of the rows of houses. These were concrete pads with cans overflowing with garbage and trash. Millions of flies were attracted to the stench. People complained, but were not careful to close the lids. Dad was happy to get the work. He bought some hip boots and followed the dump trucks to each station. After the garbage was picked up, Dad swept up what was strewn about and put it in the cans. He then took a high-powered hose and washed every corner of the stations. The superintendent said that was the best job that anyone had ever done with those garbage stations. I followed Dad like a shadow every day and watched his unbelievable dignity as he worked. I learned that any job is honorable if it is honest and makes people's lives better.

I pretty well had free rein to roam about the camp as long as I was home by dark. My Bryant cousins, Boss and Nellie, had moved into the camp and I often went over there and played with their toddler. Down the hill from the living quarters was a community building where everyone could meet. On Saturday nights they showed a movie. The first movie I remember seeing was a scary serial movie called "The Clutching Hand." This hairy. masculine hand with long claw-like nails and a tremendous grip would drift into windows of pretty girls' bedrooms and choke them to death. They always stopped the movie at an exciting point and left us hanging until the next week to find out what happened. Sometimes it took several weeks to get the whole story from the sequels. It was not unlike modern soaps on TV.

Another activity I enjoyed was the gospel singing sessions. We had an enthusiastic gentleman that would really get into the conductor part waving his arms and singing loudly. He would challenge us to sing louder and louder. Hey, I could do that. I couldn't sing so pretty, but if loud was the thing, I could do that! Some of the adult camp residents came around one night and removed him from the premises. I didn't understand their concern until I found out he was drunk.

Mr. Booth, Ray, and Clyde rented some rooms two rows up from us. Ray and Clyde didn't play with me much anymore because there were lots of little boys in the camp, and they didn't have to play with sissy girls. Mr. Booth, however, had designs on my sister, Mary. He was about 45 years old, and Mary was about sixteen. She liked him a lot and he had a car to take her places. In fact, one Sunday he took his two boys, Martha, Mary, and Lizzie across the border to Mexico. Of course, I wanted to go so badly, but they said there wasn't room for me. They came back singing songs about Mexico and talking about all the things they had seen. I was so envious! To be within 10 miles of the border and not get to see Mexico! My yearning to go there was not satisfied until about sixty years later. Mary messed up my chances when she began to cast her pretty eyes at one of the younger boys in camp. Calvin swept Mary off her feet by playing a guitar and singing to her. I had hoped Mary and Mr. Booth would get married so I would have two "brothers" to play with and someone who might take me places occasionally. It was not to happen.

At first I missed the Booth boys, but soon I made lots of other friends. Two pretty little Mexican girls lived on one of the rows. They liked to come out and play jump rope. That was one of my favorite games, too, so we hit it off quite well. Soon some of the other migrant girls told me I shouldn't play with the Mexicans. When I asked, "Why", they whispered that those girls had head lice. I had never seen a louse, so as soon as I could; I got a close up of them to make a surreptitious inspection. I saw nothing. I told my Dad what had happened, and he told me the other girls had lied to me because they were prejudiced I decided I didn't want to be prejudiced because I would miss a lot of fun, so I played with the Mexican girls as much as I wanted. Later, I heard the word "wetbacks", a negative term used for the Mexicans who swam the Rio Grande River to find work. The adult Mexicans had some choice terms for the likes of us, too. Words, I learned, have power to hurt or soothe.

My Uncle Joe Bryant made a trip back to Arkansas to sell some property. With the money from that transaction, he put in a used clothing store in Weslaco. Business was brisk. Uncle Joe was frugal, living in the back of the store to save money and keep an eye on his inventory. I liked to visit the store and watch the customers, mostly Mexicans, come and go. In the streets near the store, lively loud speakers blasted out music with exciting rhythmic beats. One popular song I especially liked was "South of the Border down Mexico Way." The hauntingly beautiful melody and lyrics stirred within me longings that I really didn't understand. Strangely enough, this most popular love song that so effectively captured the spirit of Mexico was written by an Irishman named Jimmy Kennedy along with his friend Michael Carr. It was later recorded in 1953 by Old Blue Eyes himself! (Frank Sinatra on Capitol Records)

After we had been in the camp for a while, the authorities insisted that Dad enroll Lizzie and me in school. The older kids were allowed to stay out and help Dad. Lizzie and I rode a school bus to Weslaco. It was such a big school (only one grade per room), and so much nicer than Palestine. I was overwhelmed. The teacher asked me what grade I was in. Forgetting I had been promoted to third grade, I told her second. They placed me in second grade, and I was too embarrassed to tell them when I realized what I had done. School work was a breeze. I was in the rhythm band where I played sticks. We had craft classes where I remember making a paper maiche sombrero. Good grades came easy, but I found that it was sometimes lonely at the top. Once the teacher allowed me to go outside and play on the playground because I was the only student in class who aced the spelling test. At first, I was delighted and basked in the envy I saw in the eyes of the other kids. When I got out on the playground, though, it was empty, and I had to swing by myself. I decided that was really not such a good privilege.

One Saturday when I was at the laundry room with the ladies, I was carrying my toddler cousin, James Bryant. My eye fell out of my head and broke in a million pieces on the concrete floor. I grabbed the right side of my face and let out a loud grief stricken cry. I just knew my Dad would beat me to death for this. He was always saying, "I ought to jerk your leg off and beat you to death with the bloody end of it." Those words could produce horrible graphic scenes in my head. Dad talked rough at times and laid the belt on us pretty often. I ran to find him and tell him before word got out; thinking if I told him first, he might have mercy. Instead, Dad told me it was OK and for me not to worry; we would get another eye. I loved him for understanding. He set out trying to find a place to buy another eye. He said I had grown bigger and the eye had stayed the same size, so it was too small for the socket.

Harlingen was the nearest place that had eyes. We went to an office that had drawers and drawers full of glass eyes, but none fit me. Some were the wrong color, some would look good until I blinked, then turn up into my head with only the white showing. All shipments of new eyes came from Germany, and our government had broken off trade relations with that country. It was to be well over a year before an eye could be found for me.

We stayed in Weslaco Camp seven months and five days. Regulations allowed only a year for each family. It was a facility for temporary housing until the workers could find work and a better place to stay. Martha, Mary, and Sonny, who were more attached to Mother, wanted to go back to Arkansas to see her and our sister, Ellen. They whined and begged until Dad decided to start back home. As we were going home, though, Dad wanted to go back another way up to Stigler, Oklahoma to see his sister Mary Williams whom he had not seen in twenty-six years. Since the Booths wanted to go back to Kansas, they would travel north with us.

This time we worked our way up the Texas plains near the panhandle. We would stay a few days in one place until we got money enough to move on. At one point, we were allowed to stay in a house somewhere between Brownfield and Tahokia, Texas. The watermelon harvest was just winding down, and a farmer gave dad a truck load of watermelons which he was going to store in a cellar in our back yard. When the farmer brought the truck around, our yard was so full of half-cooked flapjacks that Dad had to shovel them out of the way before he could get to the cellar to unload the truck. Dad was so embarrassed about the mess that he mouthed and raised cane for weeks about it. Even though Martha and Mary were big girls, they didn't know very much about cooking, especially on the kerosene stove without an oven.

Lizzie, Clyde, Ray, and I started back to school at a country school called West Point. We walked about two miles from our house to school. There were tumble weeds everywhere, so we decided it would be fun to drag our books to school on a tumble weed. We were to take turns pulling the weed. That worked pretty well for the first day or two, then Lizzie got mad about something and wouldn't take a turn. We told her if she wouldn't take her turn, she would have to take her books off. One word led to another until Lizzie got really angry and started shaking her finger and yelling at us. She looked so funny with her red face and shaking finger that we laughed and called her "preacher."

We pulled the tumble weed on up the road a ways, and suddenly heard a strange noise and smelled an awful stench off to the left. We were scared, but wanted to know what it was. We cautiously eased over to the place where we heard the noise, making ready to run like blazes any second. There was a cow carcass, and the growling was inside the carcass. The sides were moving. We found some dirt clods and threw at it and three opossums stuck their heads out. They had such a quizzical look with blood and fat dripping from their faces that we all laughed and started on home. We saw what looked like a dark rain cloud moving toward us in the distance. We grabbed our books and ran for the house. The cloud was not rain, but a dust storm. We got a good sandblasting before we could get inside.

School was going well until we had an assembly one day. All the students met in this large room and a guest speaker was talking. Two boys began to laugh and horseplay. The principal demanded that they behave. They let out one last nervous giggle, and the principal was back there in a flash. He grabbed one of them and slammed him against the wall. The two boys fought back and a real scuffle ensued. I was trembling. When we got home and told Dad we didn't want to go back again, he didn't force the issue.

We soon struck out again heading to Stigler, Oklahoma. We got into some pretty steep hills, and from a distance, it looked like they were blocking the highway, but as we moved closer I could see that the road curved around the mountains gradually going higher and higher. Once the Model A truck stalled and Dad turned it around and backed it up the hill. I think that model had no fuel pump but was gravity fed. We thought it funny that we were backing up the hill. I was reminded of this by a radio commercial a few years later. It was a jingle that said, "If your radiator's leaking and your motor's standing still, fill it full of Hadacol and boogy up the hill." We had boogied up the hill in reverse.

Dad stopped the first day about noon and bought some light bread. That was a really rare treat, and it was so fresh and moist. I peeled off the outside crust and ate it first, then squeezed the soft part into a ball and ate it. Sometimes we had bologna or potted meat with the bread. Pork and beans were a staple, too. Dad joked that he knew a man that went blind looking for the pork in the beans.

When we finally got to Stigler, we didn't know where my aunt lived. It was a small town so Dad began to ask if anyone knew Wesley Williams. No one knew anyone by that name. Then Dad mentioned that Wesley kept bees and sold honey. An old timer nodded and said, "Yeah, you mean the honey man!" He pointed south with a stubby finger and instructed us to take the road up "that there mountain." It was late afternoon when we arrived at Aunt Mary's house. She and her family all came running out to meet us with hugs and kisses. I remember her two girls Florence and Tea Waddy. They were about the ages of Martha and Mary. Aunt Mary told us kids to catch three of the fryer chickens in the yard, and she would fix them for supper. We chased the chickens and cornered them, then Aunt Mary wrung their necks. She dipped them in hot water to loosen the feathers, picked them, then singed the hair off them. That was standard procedure for preparing a chicken to cook. She cut the chickens open and salvaged all of the insides she could, then fed the entrails to the hungry dogs that had closely watched the whole operation.

We kids got acquainted and played while Aunt Mary fixed supper and the grownups all talked in the kitchen. That chicken smelled so good cooking it was hard to think about what we were playing. It was customary for the adults to eat first, so when the meal was ready, we still had to sit it out and wait for them. After they ate, they just sat and talked and talked while we were just salivating. Finally, they told us to come and eat. We rushed in, but had to eat from their dirty plates. The only chicken that was left was the necks, backs, gizzards, and feet. We gnawed and sucked on those and ate some biscuits. Aunt Mary made really good biscuits.

Uncle Wesley had stomach ulcers, so the doctor had prescribed goat milk for him. I tried a little of the goat milk the next morning for breakfast. It was much richer than cow's milk. We had honey, homemade butter and biscuits. That was really appreciated after the short fare of the night before. These folks were about as poor as we were and shared generously what they had for the few days we were there.

The Booths had come this far with us, but they said their good byes and left for Kansas. We stayed a couple more nights then left for Arkansas. Dad knew he had friends at Belfast who would help him. The old truck chugged along. By now, it seemed like a part of the family. Dad tried to be careful so he wouldn't get stopped without a license. The trip was iffy until we got out of the hills because we had no brakes. We kept some chunks of wood to scotch it if it picked up too much momentum. It was smooth sailing to Little Rock. We were almost home…just 35 more miles to Belfast. Dad pulled upon the Broadway Bridge and a truck was stopped in front of him. The driver was chatting to another driver. There was no way around, and we couldn't stop. The Model A ran right up under the back of the truck.

Blood rushed to my face, and I closed my eyes thinking we were all going to die. There was a big crash, water spued, and the windshield cracked. Dad got out giving us strict orders to stay put. The police came and checked the wreck. They asked Dad if he had a driver's license. He lied that he did, and luckily they didn't ask to see it. They faulted the truck driver for stopping on the bridge, and his company was to fix our truck. The problem was: What would we do and where would we stay until the truck was repaired?

We remembered that our maternal grandmother and spinster Aunt Ruth lived in Little Rock, so we located them and they agreed to put us four girls up for a few nights. Sonny Boy and Dad slept in the truck bed at the foot of the bridge. Grandma was nice to us, and seemed to be glad to have us there. She told us that if we would go back to the truck and get some clean clothes, she would take us to the movies. It must have been three or four miles back to the truck. By the time we got back, Grandma had already gone to the movies with our cousin Jimmy who lived with them. We felt betrayed. Looking back, I think she didn't have the money to take us, but it wouldn't have mattered if she had not tricked us. They had a very nice, sweet-smelling house, and I am sure we must have seemed like an invasion of wharf rats. I slept with Grandma in her room; the other girls slept on pallets. Jimmy played with me and I liked him. In a few days the truck was repaired, and we got to start home again. I think there was plenty of relief on both sides.

CHAPTER 6

Home Again to Belfast

We *rolled into Belfast, turned the corner* at Busick's store and proceeded down the road to our house. It was pretty much as we had left it except for dust and cobwebs. The house was a 40 ft. by 40 ft. structure with hewn, upright boards overlapping on the outside. There was a total of one single four-paned window on the east front, another single window for the sitting room and two sliding windows for the kitchen on the north side. These permitted such an insufficient amount of light that we never had curtains or blinds. The steep roof was made of wooden shingles that my Dad had froed (hand split) himself. Two doors in front (east side) facing the road and two doors in back (west side) provided ample entrance ways for both man and beasts. None of the doors had a knob. They were secured by a wooden pivoting latch that dropped down into a slot. The sitting room door had a string on the latch that could be fed through a small hole to the outside. That was the lock when we were away. I could well identify with Red Riding Hood's Grandmother when she said, "Lift the latch and walk in, Dear." Dad and Mom had once envisioned a dream home here, but, as the Scottish poet, Robert Burns, observed in his poem "To a Mouse", "The best laid plans of mice and men go oft astray, and leave us naught but grief and pain for promised joy." (my personal English translation.)

Inside, the rooms were in various phases of development. The original plan had included four rooms: two bedrooms, a sitting room and kitchen. The bedrooms were never partitioned, so they made one long twenty by forty foot room with only stud supports between and a big hole in the center of the ceiling for access to the attic. Walls were covered with defunct copies of the *Kansas City Star* and flattened cardboard boxes, no dry wall sealing, paint, or pretty wallpaper. Partitions separated the sitting room and the kitchen from each other and the bedrooms. Wire strung across corners served as "clothes closets."

The floors and ceilings had been constructed of green lumber from a sawmill and were roughly planed with a hand plane. When the lumber had dried, great cracks had developed, some as much as an inch across. Those floor cracks served some good purposes. One was that when it rained and the chickens ran under the house, we could feed them through the cracks. Another was that they put the fear of God and the devil in me. I had learned that God was a good Spirit and the Devil was a bad Spirit. Spirits could not be seen, but could come through cracks and walls. It seemed that the Devilish Spirit was always after me, and I feared going to sleep at night because he just might come and drag me through the cracks and take me off to some hot region to roast me on a spit like a marshmallow. I wanted to believe that the God spirit would protect me, but I knew that I hadn't been very good, so didn't expect a lot of help from Him.

Anyway, this was home, and it was nice to be back again. I couldn't wait to see what changes had occurred while we were away. Our closest neighbors were the Noble family who lived up by Busick's store. There was Granny Noble, her husband, daughter Jesse, and Wimpy her little boy who was about two. Granny also had a grown son whom she never tired of telling about. His name was Prince, and he was so handsome. Prince didn't live at home, but he visited often, and I secretly thought he was a real prince. Jesse was not home very much so Granny liked for me to come up and play with Wimpy. Granny dipped snuff, as most older ladies did then, and would pay me a nickel apiece to chew some "toothbrushes" for her. These toothbrushes were just twigs pulled from the branches of a bush. There was a little knob end where it broke off the bush. I chewed those ends until they were soft and pliable. She would then use those to dip her snuff from the box and put it between her lower lip and teeth. Her lip would pooch out in a little mound while she worked her tongue around to maneuver the dry tobacco into position.

Granny would pay me a dime to sweep under her bed or do her dishes for her. I was quite frugal and hoarded my money. One weekend Jesse's husband came. I think he was in the army. Jesse and he lay out on the lawn on a pallet quilt all day in their swimsuits with their bodies locked together. Soon he had to leave and tears rolled down their cheeks as they said goodbye. The next week Wimpy and I were playing out on the lawn.

Wimpy found what looked like an odd shaped balloon and was trying to blow it up. His spit was flying. Jesse came out of the house and jerked the "balloon" away from him and scolded him about picking up dirty things and putting them in his mouth. I thought she was making a big deal out of nothing.

Mr. Noble was foreman of a crew that made crossties, and he offered Daddy a job helping him. They shaped the ties with a broadax. He was a very good neighbor, but swore almost every breath. I had thought my Dad and his friends insulted God enough, but this man did not let up. In a few months Mr. Noble had a stroke and lost his ability to speak except for a few swear phrases. I will never forget the look of frustration and helplessness on his face as he realized he was trapped in a body that would not respond to his wishes. His eyes looked pleading like those of an animal caught in a trap. Not long after that he had another stroke and died.

Mrs. Noble was a kind, heavy-set lady. She let us come to her house to listen to her radio on nights when *Henry Aldridge* or *Digby Odell, the Friendly Undertaker* was on. To show her appreciation for my helping her, she made a couple of dresses for me on her treadle sewing machine. She cut patterns out of newspaper and fitted them, then laid them on the material. They fit so nicely, and I wore them proudly. She often got annoyed with me because I asked so many questions. She told me to keep my eyes and ears open and I would find out what I wanted to know. That didn't work quickly enough for me; I wanted instant gratification for my curiosity, but I tried to stop the questions. They just popped out of me all the time. Later, I learned that asking questions is one of the most effective ways of learning…if you don't get decapitated for doing it.

Christmas was coming up and everyone said that if little kids were good, Santa would come in the air with a big sleigh loaded with wonderful things and leave some toys and candy. I was trying really hard to be good, but every time I turned around I slipped up. I liked to play with my little cousin Phillip Van, Mrs. Busick's grandson. He was only about four. One day he threw an awful tantrum in the yard. (I suppose he was just tired) He lay down and kicked and screamed and yelled to the top of his lungs. I thought, "Uh, Oh! Santa will not visit Philip now for sure!" Wrong! When Christmas came he got a new tricycle, a ball, and a lot of nice clothes and other things. I got a few pieces of horehound candy, an apple, and an orange. Well, I decided that old bearded man didn't keep his records straight.

Kindly neighbors tried to talk to Martha because she was the oldest of us children. They told her she needed to be like a mother to Lizzie and me. Even though they meant well, that was an almost lethal thing to say. Martha's idea of being like a mother was to bark out orders...do dis, do dat...hurry up...and so on. If we did not comply instantly, she whipped us. If we made any negative remarks, she whipped us some more until we begged for mercy. I begin to be so resentful of her overbearing attitude that I became stubborn and at times vindictive. If I had realized the limitation of her mental capacity, I might have been more docile, but with my own limited capacity at the time, it may not have made any difference.

Martha was almost twelve years older than I was, and weighed about two hundred pounds. She had gotten so heavy that I would try to outrun her. She could catch me if I ran up the road where the ground was smooth, but I found out that if

I leaped the dirt clods across the plowed field, I could get away. She and Mary spent so much time talking about their dreams of their boyfriends they had in Texas that Lizzie and I were chattels. We carried water, washed dishes, made beds, slopped hogs, fed chickens, and worked in the field, but nothing was ever enough. The water was stale, the dishes weren't clean enough or I shouldn't let the dishwater run down to my elbow, the fire under the wash pot wasn't stoked properly, or the clothesline was sagging too much.

On one occasion when I was particularly obstinate, Martha grabbed me. I jerked away and ran across the field. She couldn't catch me so she went back to the house. I sat on a knoll near the church for a while, then slipped off over to Granny Noble's house. I told Granny my problem and she watched for Martha and told me to hide in her canning shelf when she saw her coming. Martha asked if I had been there and Granny lied for me. About that time Wimpy, thinking I was playing hide-and-seek, came looking for me, pulled the curtain back, and gave me away. Martha pulled me out and marched me home with my arm twisted behind my back. She got Dad's razor strop and whelped my back until the strop broke. She came to herself when the strop broke and looked at my back. She said I had better not tell Daddy or I would get more the next day. I fumed all day. I wondered what choice I really had. If she was worse tomorrow, I would be dead.

My back was swollen and hot, but I was too mad to cry. I stayed out in the yard the rest of the afternoon and waited for Dad's work truck to leave him at the store. I saw it coming and ran to meet him. I fell just before I reached him, and he hurried over to pick me up. He knew something was wrong, because

I always put on a happy face for him. I pulled my blouse up behind and showed him my back. The whelps all up and down my back had risen so I flinched at his touch. Dad said nothing but stepped off the road and began to cut a large width at least an inch in diameter from a sapling. He stripped the small limbs off with his pocket knife.

When I saw that he was going to beat Martha like she had done to me, I cried and begged him not to hurt her. She got the whipping of her life anyway, but Dad told her if I had not begged for her he would not have stopped as soon as he did. I felt ashamed that we kids were causing him problems while he was out trying to make a living for us. Coming home to Belfast was not such a good thing. Dad was with us most of the time when we worked the harvest, but now it was like a battlefield every day. I sometimes thought the little sisters in the cemetery had been spared a lot of grief.

In fact, I went on such a personal pity party that I thought I would climb the big sweet gum tree at the pet cemetery and jump out. Dad had warned me not to climb up that tree, but I thought if I were dead, I wouldn't have to worry about anybody being mad at me. I had climbed up to the lower branches before, but this time I thought I would climb to the very tip top. I climbed slowly relishing the thought of my funeral with everybody crying and remembering the many harsh things they had said and done to me. I kept climbing still determined to carry out my plan. The trunk of the tree was getting smaller and smaller. Finally, I felt that I could touch the sky as I had my legs completely wrapped around the top of the tree. All of a sudden the wind started blowing. The flimsy tree top began swaying and I was afraid it was going to break. Then I asked myself, "Why am I clinging like a scared kitten?" I had turned to all arms and legs wrapping around the slender top. So tightly did I cling that even my neck was curved in the shape of the swaying tree top. Hey, didn't I plan to jump? Then, it occurred to me...what if no one cried or really cared? What if I should not die, but just be terribly crippled? "Wait a minute, let me see," my little Texas friend's words echoed in my head. Maybe this was not such a swell idea, after all! Slowly, very slowly and carefully I inched my way back down the tree. I gave a sigh of relief when I reached the lower familiar branches and threw a sweet gum ball at Donald Cullins as he passed on the road beneath me. He looked around startled, laughed, picked it up, and threw it right back at me. We both missed, but it didn't matter.

In the spring, Dad bought an old horse. He taught Martha to plow. I was to go behind her and drop the seed. Mary and Lizzie stayed at the house to clean and cook. Mary and I were easier to get along with than Martha and Lizzie, so he divided the chores to put me with Martha and Mary with Lizzie. Martha hitched up old Maude every morning and laid off rows for me to plant. I was to drop corn or pea seeds, and then she would come back and cover them. One day in the late afternoon when I was especially hot and tired, I buried a bunch of the seed around a stump. I then reported that I was out of seed. In a couple of weeks the seeds started sprouting and that stump came back from the dead. It was green all over, but the greenery looked suspiciously like corn seedlings. I really caught the dickens. Dad couldn't stand waste because everything was so hard to come by. His philosophy was to thrash the devil out of us when we did something wrong. If that didn't straighten us out, he had plenty more where that came from. There was none of the modern "time out" or loss of privileges…we had no privileges. He would never withhold food either by making us go to bed hungry.

Martha did not try to whip me anymore, but she had a sharp tongue. I didn't realize how limited she was in her ability to cope and grew resentful toward her tantrums and overbearing personality. One wash day was particularly typical of how we clashed. Martha and I were to fill the big, black wash pot with water and build a fire under it. To get the water, we had to carry water in a number three wash tub from the well which was about 50 yards from the house. We grabbed the empty tub by the handles and swung it between us on the way up to the well. We laughed and talked. She was rather good at whistling a tune, and I was learning pretty fast through imitating her. We tried that together. "Camp Town Races" was one of our favorites and always put us in a good mood, especially the "Do Dah" part.

We reached the well, and Martha took the galvanized bucket off its peg on the well post and lowered it down into the water. I went around to the opposite side of the wooden curb and tiptoed so I could see over the edge to watch the bucket gurgle as it filled with water. She brought it up and emptied it into the tub. The bucket went down again and I wandered nearby to chase frogs and butterflies until she was ready for me to help her carry the tub. Soon she called, and I hurried back to help her.

The tub was full almost to overflowing! I knew it would be heavy, but she was adamant and insisted the more we carried per trip, the fewer trips we would have to make. We each took our respective handles and lifted. She took no account of the difference in our heights and strengths, so her side went up higher than mine. Water spilled over my bare feet and onto the ground. Impatiently she yelled, "Raise you side eyer, Stoopid!" That stung me a little, but I lifted a little higher so the water did not spill out the second try. We started forward, but only advanced a few feet until the weight of the water caused the handle to press into and hurt my hand. "Rest a minute," I panted as I plumped the tub down to rub the painful imprint in my hand. Water splashed again, and her patience wore thinner. We changed sides and tried again. The same thing happened.

"Come on," she spat at me, "or we won't eber git troo wid de warshing."

"You filled it too full," I whined. "I can't carry it like that." I kicked the tub a disgusted little kick.

"You 'er just a lazy 'ittle shit! She retorted. "Git yore side 'en come on."

The word "shit" stung me invoking images of the sights and smells of our outhouse. I called her a maggot, and she threatened to hit me. I didn't think she would after the razor strop incident, but by that time I didn't care. We were both angry, and she began to cuss so bad I expected God to strike her with lightning in broad daylight. She had more practice at that sort of thing than I had and a much larger vocabulary of clandestine words. She also had me bested in volume. I felt at a great disadvantage, so I cast about in my mind for a way to even the score.

Suddenly a barrage of bad words that I had heard my dad and other men folk use surfaced, and I felt power! Of course

I knew that those words were reserved only for men. Their use gave men macho and status! I was told they would make women look cheap and stupid and would rot their teeth. Men didn't have to think or be reasonable…just yell them out with the force of an incantation, and things happened. (So effective!) The few times I had ventured to use even one of the mildest of them, I was quickly put in "my place" by the nearest, well-meaning, self-righteous adult.

This occasion, however, called for extreme measures. I needed to haul out the "big guns." I glanced furtively around to see if anyone was near…."Safe enough!" I thought, and out they came like a flaming burst from the mouth of a dragon. I scorched her with "fatso, wench, bitch, mulligrubber," and other unspeakable things. (I was careful not to bring God into this, though, because I didn't want Him to come out against me, too.) Martha stopped in her tracks and stared at me. She was speechless! Her mouth flew open and her buck teeth protruded like an ass. Wow, I was awesome!

Then she slowly pulled herself together and matched my outburst with an even bigger one of her own. We pulled out all the stops. For at least ten minutes we left the tub unattended and hurled insults at each other. Suddenly from out of nowhere, Daddy appeared like the Master in "The Sorcerer's Apprentice." Our broomstick words fell flat as we backed away from Daddy's raised arm. He thrashed us unmercifully with his leather belt, (no questions asked, no explanations forthcoming). Then worst of all, he made us kiss and make up. What a disgusting kiss! I would rather have bitten off her nose. We cowed down the rest of the day without incident except for the fiery looks between us. I later crawled off to lick my wounds and ponder the lesson

I learned. I was truly ashamed of the things I had said. To this day, I am hesitant to use any of those words I used so freely on that occasion.

By this time Sonny Boy was working away from home at Bauxite. He came home late one night very sick. Dad sent me to Uncle Joe's store to get some Dr. Tichnor's antiseptic. He would put a few drops of it in water to help an upset stomach. When I got back with the medicine, Sonny had put his foot across the table and knocked it over, breaking the kerosene lamp. He had vomited all over himself and the floor. It turned out, Sonny was just drunk. I guessed that was part of the "wild oats" young men were supposed to sow.

Another time we were all at the supper table talking about the day's events when Sonny Boy came in with a friend he introduced as Curtis Walters. He was red headed with freckles and a winning smile. Sonny was trying to be the matchmaker for Martha, but Curtis fell for Mary. Soon Mary and Curtis were married, and Dad gave his blessing. Martha soon found her a feller. I was never sure how they met, but he was a guy from Benton named Russell Stancil. Sonny Boy hung out with our cousin Boss Bryant most of the time because he had taken a shine to Boss' wife's pretty sister, Betty Sue Earnest. They were soon married. All these changes took place over a relatively short time and by the spring of 1942 Lizzie and I were in charge of the house. Now we must be more responsible!

Lizzie awoke one morning in late March and wanted me to help her burn off the sage grass on our garden spot so we could start a garden. I went out to help her, but the wind was whipping up and I figured it was too dangerous. I thought I had persuaded her to wait, so I went back into the house and settled down with a good Grace Livingston Hill book (these were innocent dreamy love stories). I could hear her mumbling something about me being lazy, but paid no attention. Just as I reached an exciting part of the book, Lizzie came running up and breathlessly panted that she had let fire get out, and it was sweeping across our sage grass field toward the woods and houses over there. I ran to get some toe sacks and wet them at the well, then hurried to the fire line and started beating out the flames. The heat was so intense that I was making little headway. I was so scared and mad with Lizzie at the same time.

A few neighbors, who happened to be home, saw our plight and hurried over to help us. They fired against the wood line hoping to burn a path before the big blazes reached that far. The people who lived in the house began emptying out their belongings and carrying them across the gravel road that led to the church. We were losing the battle.

Suddenly out of nowhere it seemed, a caravan of army vehicles rolled in to Belfast. It was from the Civilian Conservation Corps camp about five or six miles away around what is now Ico. They had spotted the fire from the forest tower and had come to help. Those jeeps were loaded with CCC recruits who were trained well for such an occasion. They fanned out in all directions and beat flames with green pine saplings. It was like a western movie where the cavalry arrived in the nick of time. Soon the fire was reduced to a few embers and smoke. No real harm done! The guys came by our well for a drink of water before they left, and I thought, "What a fine bunch of unattached guys. Maybe I would marry one of them someday!" I thanked them over and over again, and they just smiled and looked at me curiously. When I went back to the house and caught a glimpse of myself in the mirror, I was horrified. My hair was singed and my face streaked with soot and tears. My clothes were dirty and ragged. What a sight! No wonder the guys had looked at me curiously, maybe pityingly. I would have to look better than that if anyone should ever find me attractive! (I have later thanked God many times for Roosevelt's New Deal program that provided work for thousands of young men and made it possible for these men to assist us on that occasion.)

Almost a year passed after we returned to Arkansas, and Dad had finally managed to get me another eye. It didn't fit very well, but was better than a hole in the head. I had not been to school since the incident at West Point. Palestine school had consolidated with Sheridan while we were gone, and now the students were bused all the way to Sheridan, about 11 miles from where we lived. One day I was watching when the school bus let off the Belfast kids at Busick's store. Virginia Harrington was among those emerging from the bus. Virginia was always outgoing and very talkative. She yelled and waved goodbye to those on the bus, and they waved out the windows to her. What a joyful sound and what a profound effect those kids had on me without being aware of it. They all looked so cheerful that it set me to thinking how I might be missing out on some good times. That night I asked Dad if I could go to school. He said I could if I wanted. Lizzie decided to go, too, so the next morning we caught the school bus that we dubbed "the chicken coop".

CHAPTER 7

Back to School

Going to Sheridan School really marked a turning point in my life. I was nine years old and in the third grade. Lizzie had failed and was supposed to be in fourth grade. She told school officials she was in the sixth, and they put her in the class with her classmates she had had at Palestine. She struggled all the way through her senior year. I blossomed. Mrs. Eades, my teacher, put me in charge of tutoring the slow readers when we had reading time. She made hot chocolate for our whole class on cold days. I learned to play all kinds of games at recess. One of my favorite games similar to a dance was called Jimmy Crack Corn. Others were Drop the Handkerchief, Farmer in the Dell, Go in and out the Windows, Jump Rope, Hopscotch, and Jacks. Some girls and I often played school at recess with one being the teacher and the others reciting lessons. I liked basketball, but the tall girls in my class liked to play "keep away". I was short and limited by my vision so was not very successful at that. I remember one of the best basketball players was Marilyn Sue Hope. When we chose sides, I always hoped she would choose me. (She sometimes did if I was the only one left.)

Mrs. Eades took our class to the public library about once a month. It was in an old log lodge building about three blocks from our campus. I checked out all the books they would let me have. It was from those books I learned a lot of Greek mythology. I didn't learn until much later what a great influence the Greeks culture and society had on our own. For the present, I was satisfied to enjoy the imaginative stories. Some of my favorites were stories of metamorphosis where lovers would die but then turn into beautiful nightingales and get to live together indefinitely. I liked Orpheus who went down into Hades looking for his beloved. He sang and played so beautifully for her that the rocks and trees shed tears of empathy. Even Pluto, the god of the underworld, was moved by his petition. I thought it would be wonderful if someone could love me that completely.

Hercules was my fantasy hero because he was so strong that he choked the life out of two snakes that crawled into his baby bed. I wondered why Helen, the most beautiful woman in the world, was unfaithful to her husband who loved her so dearly and caused a ten-year war in which so many people were killed. (Of course the Greeks excused her behavior by saying the god Aphrodite made her do it, but I didn't buy that.) Even though I was impressionable and saturated my mind with romance and idealism, I was still jarred from reverie by the real world around me. I read the tall tales of Paul Bunyan and his Big Blue Ox because my Dad was a timber worker and had related many tall tales he had heard among the loggers. I especially liked the railroad story of John Henry who was determined to beat the new fangled jack hammer that threatened to destroy his way of life as many of the technology inventions have done to people in recent years.

As I got a little older, a neighbor boy, Donald Cullins and I shared comic books. We read Donald Duck, Porky and Petunia Pig, and the Marvel comics about Wonder Woman and Super Man. The latter two were my role models because they fought for right and justice. I saved every penny I could to buy more comic books. They cost five cents each, so I could get ten for fifty cents. Donald bought all he could, and we could hardly wait to swap out when we finished reading a batch. Once I discovered the joy of reading, I wanted to read everything.

There was such a stark contrast between school and home. School was like a magic world of escape, so whether it was reading or playing, it was all fun. My teachers were all so kind and encouraging.

It was about this time our school got a cafeteria. We loaded on a bus and rode over to the basement of Mckenzie Hall where they served a good hot lunch. They served dishes I had never seen before. My very favorite was their meat loaf. I could have eaten my weight in that. Also the ladies made yeast rolls from scratch that were as light and fluffy as air. My enjoyment of that was to be short lived however. One day I walked through the door where the girls were taking lunch tickets. I was talking to my friends and forgot to give them my ticket. I advanced almost to the place where we got the food trays and looked down to see I still had my ticket in my hand. I told my friend and she said, "Let it go, you can use it tomorrow." I couldn't do that, so I stepped out of line and went back to give the girls my ticket.

When I came back up and got in line where I had left out, the superintendent came tearing up and grabbed my ear and told me to get back to the end of the line. Kids were always trying to break line and he thought that was what I was doing. He was so gruff and had such a firm grip on my ear that I froze with a lump in my throat. He literally pushed me back down the line. When we got back to where the ticket takers were, they explained to him. He didn't apologize, but gruffly told me "to get back up there then." I was humiliated and crying and stubbornly insisted on going to the end of the line. He would have none of that and walked me back up there himself, made me get a tray, and sat down opposite me to see that I did eat. The food stuck in my throat. I could not swallow. He finally let me go, and I cried most of the afternoon. I would never go back to the lunchroom. I have thought many times later what a lot of wonderful meals I missed because of my stubbornness. When I became a teacher at the high school years later, I went to the lunchroom almost every day. I learned, too, that administrators and teachers make mistakes like everyone else, and I should have been more forgiving.

In December of 1941, World War II broke out. The Japanese bombed our ship base at Pearl Harbor, Hawaii. Our country was ill prepared for the attack but now had no choice but to defend our homeland. Germany and Italy had joined forces with Japan, (Axis) and those three countries were sweeping Europe and the Far East. The fighting was fierce overseas and many young men were called up by the draft board to serve the country. We had a radio by that time and Dad listened to every news broadcast. I liked to hear President Roosevelt speak encouraging words. We got graphic, up-to-date detail on the progress of the war including how many men were killed or wounded in each hot zone every day. Hitler was pictured as a mad man who wanted control of the whole world. I began to have horrible dreams of armies marching through our area and shooting everyone they could see. I would wake shaking with fright from my imagination. To make matters worse for me, I heard one soldier on leave talking about having a pickled Jap's ear in a jar in his barracks. Mrs. Gladys McBurnett, a lady from our church, always implored everyone to pray for her twin sons Coy and Roy who were in the conflict.

I liked the sharp uniforms of the army, marines, and air corps. They sported crisp creased trousers and shiny shoes. Some of the most rustic looking farm boys suddenly became gentlemen with a purpose. They squared their shoulders and marched away. I even harbored ambitions of joining the WACS or the WAVES when I got old enough. The war songs stirred me and made me feel patriotic, especially the Air Force song "Of we go, into the wild blue yonder, Climbing high into the sun. Down we go, zooming to meet our thunder, Atta boy, give 'er the gun, give 'er the gun. Rat-a tat, tat a tat tat…" My paraphrase of the words changed with each rendition, but I sang that with zest and expression (when alone). Young boys played soldier instead of cowboys now.

For me, all the romance and glorification of war culminated with Sonny Boy getting the draft call. He was my only brother. I prayed so hard that he would not have to go. I was so afraid he would come home in a body bag. He went for an examination, but got a notice that he was 4-F. I don't know why he did not pass, but was thankful he was spared. Some young men found out they would be deferred if they were married with a family, so many of them rushed their wedding dates and started a family as quickly as possible. As the war dragged on for over four years, though, almost all the men had to take a turn. Belfast contributed many young men to the service, but most of them returned and reaped the benefits of their country's gratitude. I often wondered if the Axis group had won the war if we would now be speaking Japanese or German. Also if their countries would have helped rebuild ours as we did theirs. I felt sorry that many Japanese American citizens were stripped of all they owned and taken to holding camps because the government feared they might cause harm to other citizens. I thought it too bad that we could not look into people's hearts and know how they really felt. I heard my dad talking about one such camp in Arkansas.

On the home front, everybody was trying to help. We collected scrap iron, tin, paper…anything that could be used in the war effort. Food and clothes, gas, and almost everything was rationed. Teachers gave out little packs of seeds at school and encouraged all the children to plant "Victory Gardens." I remember Mrs. Wilma Thornton, my very favorite teacher, encouraged us to save our money and buy war stamps which we kept in a stamp book. These could be redeemed for cash with interest after a certain time lapse. Mrs. Thornton awarded me my first stamp for a history scrapbook I made for her class. The train running by our house now began carrying several coaches with troops. I would stand outside and wave at them until the train was out of sight. The soldiers gathered at the windows and hundreds of hands were waving back to me. Sometimes they threw me some gum, candy, or K-rations.

.When I passed to the fourth grade, my class moved over to the old Missionary Baptist College Building that now housed the fourth, fifth, and sixth grades. I had a reading teacher named Rundell who was very strict. She drilled us with the dictionary. We must have proper pronunciation. Her vowel sounds were Ah, A, E, O, and OO similar to the New England dialect. We were grounded in the A, E, I, O, U sounds. We secretly belittled her, but she commanded our respect. She gave frequent standardized reading tests and worked very hard to bring us up to standard. I appreciate her for that now.

Mrs. Stockburger was my fifth grade geography teacher. The trip to Texas had whetted my appetite for geography, and I wanted to learn more and more about other places with hope of someday getting to see some more of them. I learned to read maps and find out what kinds of products were produced in different places. Also, I kept reading stories about the children who lived there and what they experienced. I once heard a song about "Far Away Places" that expressed my feelings: Some of the words were; "I am going to China or maybe Siam, I want to see for myself, All those far away places with the strange sounding names in a book that I took from a shelf."

That year at Christmas my class drew names. I drew Bill Barnes' name. I knew Bill because his dad was the ice man and Bill had often rode the ice truck with his dad to deliver ice. We were to spend about fifty cents for a gift. As usual, money was scarce around our house and fifty cents was about a day's work for my dad when work was available. I didn't know how I would get a gift for Bill, and had no idea what he would like.

My dad came to the rescue again. He whittled a lot when he was relaxing and made some six-piece puzzle balls. He said he thought a boy would like one of those. He gave me one about the size of a baseball. I painted it with brown shoe polish and wrapped it in tissue paper for Bill. I didn't want to put my name on it in case he didn't like it.

Bill's eyes lit up when he saw the ball and he remarked how unusual it was. Some of the kids ran over to have a look and in the commotion that followed, it came apart. Bill took the pieces home and when asked what he got, he told his parents he got a ball, but it had come apart. One person said he didn't believe those little sticks were a ball and bet Bill a dollar he couldn't make a ball of them. Bill was always one for a good challenge, so he set about trying to prove his story. As he told us later, he and one of his sisters worked half the night putting those pieces in every imaginable shape until they finally got it back together. He came back to school waving his dollar bill. That was a lot of money to us, and Bill was quite the hero. I don't remember that I ever told him where the ball came from.

Mrs. Harris, our principal, taught me fifth and sixth grade math. I learned about addition, subtraction, fractions and powers. (Did not yet learn how to do square root) Math seemed like a game to me because I was not connecting its importance to real life. Nevertheless, I soaked it up like a sponge. We played dominoes a lot at home, and I think that helped me to learn much about numbers.

My little sister, Ellen, started to school when I entered fifth grade. Aunt Cora tried to enroll her as Helen Marie Tribble because she liked the name Helen and thought Ellen should have a middle name like everyone else. The school principal knew Ellen was my sister and asked me about it. They said her records might get mixed up if she didn't enroll under her real name, so she came to school as Ellen Pierce. The Tribbles still like to call her Helen to this day, and it was a tribute to her that they accepted her. Ellen always had very pretty dresses (Aunt Cora was an excellent seamstress), and her hair was so lovely. She would try to follow me around at recess. At first I was glad to have her with me since we had never spent much time together, but then she started to acting superior when the other kids would tell her how pretty she was. She would toss her curls and say, "I know it! I am the prettiest one in my family!" Even though it was true, I didn't much like to hear it because I already felt like an ugly duckling.

Another blow to my ego came later that year when our class was going to do a historical skit about Lewis and Clark's expedition to explore the Louisiana Purchase. My part was to participate in a group square dance with Bobby Joe Haralson being my partner. That was the age when boys were still shy and afraid of being teased. Bobby Joe looked at me and said he wasn't going to dance with no girl. I was embarrassed and thought I was a reject. The teacher worked it out and Bobby came around, but then another problem developed. The girls were to dress like pioneer women wearing a sun bonnet and calico dress. Dad bought me a dress at Busick's store. It was quite long and probably would have been just fine, but I was determined to shorten it. It made me feel like an old woman. The skirt was cut on the bias, and when I tried to tear off a bit of the hem, it didn't tear straight and the skirt was hiked up on one side. The teacher loaned me a bonnet which I washed, starched and ironed myself. What with the rejection from

Bobby Joe and the dorky clothes, I had a bad feeling about the whole thing. My love for the stage soon overcame that, however, when the music played and we were the "Buffalo Gals dancing to the light of the moon."

By sixth grade, I had advanced in my reading to the Ladies Birthday Almanac. I wanted to know about zodiac signs and how people knew when to plant certain crops. On one page, I found an advertisement for some cream that was supposed to enhance the breast. It hadn't occurred to me that a girl needed big breasts, but the picture made it look glamorous. My own had begun to grow a little, but were a little sore to the touch. I turned my attention to those bumps and wondered how big they were going to get. I wanted to be pretty and look nice, but it seemed to me that if they got very big, they would flop around in my way. I wore a sweater to school one day and noticed that the bumps were protruding a bit. Mrs. Harris called me over in motherly privacy and whispered, "Honey, you need to wear a bra." I flushed a deep red, but thanked her.

How in the world was I going to get a bra? I sure was not going to ask my Dad about that. Where would I get money for a bra? I almost thought my body had betrayed me by causing such a dilemma. I looked around our house and found some clean white feed sacks, so I decided to try to make one. I carefully cut a pattern out of newspaper as I had seen Granny Noble do a few years back, shaped the paper around those budding breasts, and then pinned the pattern to the cloth. It took a whole day to stitch it by hand, but I did it. It didn't fit any too well, but gave me a little lift.

At the end of sixth grade year, Mrs. Harris came into our room and announced that I was class valedictorian. I had no idea what that meant, but the big word made me wonder if I had done something wrong. The kids all looked at me and suddenly burst out in cheers. That meant that I would have to give a speech at our graduation. Marilyn Sue Hope was the salutatorian and would follow my speech with one prepared for her. I really felt humbled for the honor because I knew that several in the class were smarter and had more well-rounded personalities than I did.

The best thing about graduation was that everybody started giving me presents. It was better than Christmas. I suddenly changed from a nobody to an intelligent being. My Dad bought me a bicycle, Mrs. Kelly gave me a small book entitled *Abundant Living* that was filled with good spiritual advice and simple prayers, Mrs. Busick gave me some nice cologne and a pretty blouse. Mrs. Harris gave me a gift box with five pairs of panties (no bra). Sue Mathews' mother gave me a cream colored pinafore dress that was as soft and smooth as a powder puff. She gave me a sheer green polk-a-dot blouse to wear under it and bought me some brand new black, patent leather, wedge-heeled sandals. Those sandals made me feel tall, and were the top of teenage fashion statement. Together that was to be my graduation outfit. We didn't wear cap and gown like the seniors.

My cousin, Delma Hendon was a beautician who offered to give me a free perm and hair style. I had never had a perm so thought that would be really cool. I had a surprise coming because perms were given using a strange contraption of a machine with wires attached to each curl. It was almost as scary as being in the electric chair. She rolled my hair and hooked me up. There was a buzzing sound and I could smell hair cooking. I jumped out of the chair, but Delma grabbed me and held me down assuring me that it was ok. Delma took a fan and blew on my head while the perm was processing. It would get too hot one place then another as she tried to cool it. Finally she took off the electric wires and unwound my hair. Cheeze! Did I have curl! You couldn't tell which ends were stuck in the head. My hair was dry as a wood chip and my head was sore. Delma styled it so pretty, though, that I felt like a princess.

After I returned home, and had to do my hair myself, I washed it, and a lot of it fell out. I had plenty left, though, because my hair was quite thick. I didn't know how to style it like Delma had done, so it just puffed out all over my head. I think I must have had one of the first Afros ever. I tried taming it a little by rolling it on paper-wrapped metal strips that I cut from a Prince Albert tobacco can. That just made it even more kinky. Then some of my friends told me that I would get a softer look by cutting kotex into inch strips and rolling my hair on those. That worked better. The curls were softer, but required more brushing to get the fuzz and lint of the strips out. I decided it sure was a lot of trouble to try to look pretty.

Graduation day came and my Dad came by the school to bring me something I had left at home. Mrs. Harris insisted he stay for the ceremony. He was a little embarrassed because he was wearing some spotted overalls. Lizzie and I had tried to get the pine resin out of them by dousing them with purex before we washed them. They were brand new overalls, and we had made spots all over them. The teacher persuaded Dad to stay anyway, so he backed up in a remote corner and waited. I was so proud that he got to hear my speech. Most of the other kids had parents there, and I had felt a little left out before he came. I had always tried hard so he would be proud of me, and this day was like his crowning glory instead of mine.

The summer after graduation, Sue Matthews invited me to come stay with her and attend Bible school at the First Baptist Church. I had never gone to Bible School, but loved to go to church and Sunday School at Belfast Missionary Baptist Church near my house. Mr. W.O. Parks was our pastor, but he pastured several churches and only came to Belfast once a month. Other Sundays we met for a devotional lesson and sang songs. I loved that old *Favorite Songs and Hymns* paper back hymnal and knew about two-thirds of the songs by heart. Verdieree Cullins, my regular Sunday School teacher, taught us from some colorful story cards. I remember learning the Ten Commandments. The more I thought about those, the more I realized how impossible it was for me to keep all of them. I felt doomed to a hot hell, but still had love and respect for Jesus and prayed to Him all the time. Just maybe He would have mercy and just let me stand on the edge of Heaven and peep through a hole in a cloud or something. I deeply desired to be good like I thought other people were, but I thought I was probably a hopeless case.

The two weeks of Bible School were a mixed bag. The Matthews home was very nice, and Sue's mother would run bath water for me to bathe every evening, no carrying from a well, it just ran out a faucet. ("So this was what it was like to have a mother," I thought.) She had some floral towels on a rack that I thought were too pretty to use, so when I got out of the tub, I dried off on my dirty clothes. Mrs. Mathews seemed disappointed that I did not use the towels. I didn't tell her that we had no towels or wash cloths at home. I helped with the dishes gladly, while Sue, Tiny, and Dot had to be persuaded with promises of rewards. Mrs. Matthews washed my clothes every day. Their way of life was so different from mine that I felt out of place and didn't know how to adjust. During the day, I smiled, but at night I cried softly into my pillow. I was so grateful for their generosity, but didn't know how to express my feelings.

Bible School was great! Brother L. D. Foreman was pastor. He was a powerful speaker. He pleaded with us to repent of our evil ways and be saved forevermore. It was so convincing, but at the same time confusing. Bobbie Nelson, a young Methodist girl, came to Bible School. I found it common for the children of different denominations to visit the Bible School of other churches. I remember Bobbie as a friendly girl with a wide smile. Our lives were to cross in many ways after that.

One afternoon after Bible School, Sue and I went with some other girls over to see Nancy Harris. While there, we played cards. I knew about playing cards…rummy, poker, solitaire, coon can, old maid, etc. Some of the church people that I knew frowned on playing cards, so I pretended I didn't know much about them. We all had a lovely time together that afternoon. I knew a lot of winning strategies, but threw almost every game so as not "to blow my cover.' I thought I was too crude for these pretty, cultured girls.

I had admired Sue since we were in third grade together. She took voice lessons, and would recite poems with such expression and clarity that I yearned to do the same. I began to memorize lots of poems and would stand on a stump in the pasture and recite them to the curious animals.

The week passed so quickly, and I was amazed at how many of my questions about God were answered. When it was time for me to go home, Sue's mother gave me a book of illustrated Bible Stories. I read it cover to cover many times. I thought of all the Bible people as ordinary people with struggles like my own, and I took courage in the fact that God guided and led them. I wished for a little cloud to guide me. I really loved all those people from the church and Sue's home for their kindness.

That summer, Lizzie and I were home alone most of the time. I enjoyed nettling her and getting her all worked up then backing off and laughing at her. One afternoon, I went out the back door, eased quietly around the house and knocked on the front door to make her think someone had come to see us. As she was coming to open the door, I would run around to another side of the house. I repeated this three or four times until she was getting riled. I decided that was enough fun for now, and went to the store to get myself a coke. When I started back, I saw a tin can by the side of the road and gave it a kick forward. I entertained myself all the way home with the can. As I reached the yard gate and opened it, I saw the biggest black man I had ever seen. He was sitting in the yard eating biscuits. I wondered where Lizzie was and if he had hurt or maybe killed her. I eased the gate shut and flew back up the road. I circled around the field and quietly entered the back door looking for Lizzie. She was huddled in the kitchen and said, "I ought to kill you!"

The black man, a hobo from the railroad track, had stopped to ask for something to eat. When he knocked on the door, Lizzie, tired of my silly game, said, "Come in!" He knocked again, and she said the same in a little louder, more annoyed voice. On the third knock she was so exasperated that she grabbed a broom and ran to the door. She swung it open and said, "If you don't get yourself on in here, I am going to punch you with this...." Her voice trailed as her eyes started at the feet of the stranger, then took in the whole of his stature. He politely asked for food, and she had given him the biscuits and some water. He thanked her kindly and insisted on chopping some stow wood for the favor. Lots of hobos came down the track. Dad had always instructed us to feed them. They never tried to hurt us. He told us about signs they used to know where they could get food. We could sometimes see them riding in or on top of boxcars. I often wondered where they came from and where they were going.

By this time Grandma Tribble lived with Aunt Cora and Uncle Bud. Aunt Cora took in all the stray people, not only Ellen and Grandma, but also a bachelor brother of hers. I never heard her complain even though it must have been hard. Grandma sent word that she would visit us one day. Aunt Cora would bring her when she took Uncle Bud to work at the Sheridan sawmill. She would get to stay until late afternoon when Aunt Cora would pick her up. Lizzie and I really scurried around the day before scrubbing the floors, changing the beds and cleaning places we hadn't touched in a long time. Our oil cloth on the table was worn, so we covered it with a feed-sack sheet. That morning she was to arrive, we were eager to see her, but yet a little reticent because we had not been around her enough to feel comfortable or know what to say. It was almost noon when she got there and we had a "nice" meal prepared for her... fresh English peas from the garden, fried potatoes, corn bread, apple cobbler, and tea. We saw the car coming up the road and ran to greet her. She emerged with her arms loaded with things for us. Inside she showed us quilt tops she had pieced for each of us. She loved to piece quilt tops and made some lovely designs.

She didn't realize that neither Lizzie nor I knew how to quilt, but it really didn't matter. She cared enough to do it. She had also made homemade cookies. We talked a bit then led her into the kitchen to eat lunch. She sat so erect in her chair and complimented us on such a nice meal. She folded her hands and said a blessing. Everything was going fine until a strong puff of wind came and blew black soot through the ceiling cracks. Soot had accumulated in the attic from the wood stoves and now covered our food. It was nothing new to us. We just raked the soot gently aside and began to eat. Grandma's smile turned upside down. She could not eat the food, but suggested we eat the cookies she had brought. Grandma never visited us again.

Grandma T

CHAPTER 8

High School

September came and seventh grade for me. I would go across town to the high school. High school was so different. We changed classes every hour, and had to keep our books in metal lockers. The State Department of Education mandated that we have physical education with our studies. At first all the students went outside, but that posed a problem when the weather was bad. Soon the school erected the Kelly-Williams Gymnasium. This building served a multipurpose. The gym was in the center with classrooms around it on upper and lower floors. It had a catwalk around the upper floor on the gym side, and all the lockers were placed up there making it necessary for almost all the students to go there between classes. We had bad traffic jams, so Mr. Mckenzie ruled that all traffic should move right around the catwalk. That was almost as big a problem to monitor as the cafeteria line. It amazed me how Mr. Mckenzie could be everywhere at the same time. He could still put the fear of the devil into everyone except the most hardened characters by yanking his belt off quick as a flash and warping it against a table or chair. (I secretly wished his pants would fall down so his bald head would turn red. I imagined he had never suffered any humiliation in his life.)

I really enjoyed physical education. We played table tennis, volleyball, and a number of group games. The activity I liked best was square dancing, but the area churches soon put an end to that as being sinful. It seemed it was all right to play any game as long as you did not have music with it. I liked the music and for the life of me could not see what harm we were doing.

Soon the powers that be decided we must have sex education. Our gym teacher Mr. Jim Zimmerman was in charge of teaching that. He sent the boys to a separate room, and then quite red-faced and obviously nervous, he turned on a movie about ovulation and menstrual periods and left the room. We thought it was so funny that he was so embarrassed that we giggled all through the short movie and paid little attention to it. He later became an excellent high school principal with a gruff exterior, but a heart of gold.

To save the district money in the way of a teacher's salary, Mr. McKenzie instituted an honor study hall. The study hall was on the west side of the gym's upper floor. The school library was in the north end of the study room. If a student wanted a book, he/she wrote the name of the book or author and passed it to the librarian. We didn't get to browse the stacks. The book was brought out and the student signed for it. The honor study hall was based on every student being responsible for reporting any student seen talking or misbehaving. The student reported for whispering or even looking around, would receive an F in conduct. Sometimes it felt like the Nazi or Russian secret police was spying on us. The conduct grades appeared on report cards and were the most humiliating of any punishment one could get. I was determined to keep a good record, so if I finished all my class homework, I would read the encyclopedias that were shelved outside the library area. We had free access to those, and I learn a lot of incidental things that served me well in my classes.

We had a student government complete with a president, vice president, secretary, and representatives elected from each grade--seven through twelve. Mrs. Wilma Thornton, the sponsor, held daily meetings in her homeroom. They planned assemblies of about thirty minutes each which would be presented in McKenzie Hall Auditorium right after lunch each day. Another of their duties was to hold court sessions for students who were reported for misconduct. The loud speakers in every room would announce for students to report to Mrs. Thornton's room immediately. Everyone knew who was in trouble. One day my name was called. My heart thumped hard in my chest, and my knees were so shaky that I could hardly walk the "Green Mile" to the slaughter. Meanwhile, I tossed about in my memory to try to think what I might have done wrong. When I got to Mrs. Thornton's room, I peeked inside cautiously. No one was there but Mrs. Thornton herself. She smiled a sweet smile and told me to come in. She had some clothes for me that her daughter, Betty Lou had outgrown. They were very nice and most appreciated, but I think she never realized how close she came to giving me a heart attack.

It was in high school that I began to notice what a disadvantage the bus students had from those who lived near school. Most of our parents had no transportation, so we did not get to participate in many extracurricular activities. I longed to be in the band or chorus, but much of their practice was after school. Many of my friends wanted me to run for student council, but that, too, often required after school involvement. One year, I ran anyway because a friend put my name on petition and got a required number of signatures. I got the most votes in the primary, but since I didn't have a majority, I lost in the ensuing runoff. It was fun anyway. I got to make campaign speeches to the whole student body.

I had continued my love for reading, and enjoyed getting to share with the class in a monthly book report. Mrs. McCoy was my English teacher who encouraged me to read lots of books. Once though, she was not too pleased with the type of book I reported on. It was a "paperback"! All paperbacks at that time were considered trashy reading by the educated elite, not necessarily for their content, but just because they were paperbacks. I had read a story about a man who had gone to Paris. He visited a Turkish bath. Just as he was relaxing in the steam, a mouse ran through and frightened him. He grabbed a towel, wrapped it quickly around him and ran down the street hollering at the top of his voice. I thought the scene was funny mostly because it seemed ludicrous that a grown man would be scared of a mouse, and I described it to the class in detail. They laughed and laughed. Mrs. McCoy reprimanded me for that one and said I shouldn't read things like that. I thought I saw a glimmer of a smile on her face though.

Mrs. McCoy had been to Mexico and brought some of her souvenirs to show the class. They were mostly pottery with designs made by the Indians there. There was always a bird design and snakes and lizards. I later learned that those things were sacred to some of the tribes. For the most part they didn't consider the snake to represent evil like we did in our culture. My earlier trip to Texas made her talk delightful to me.

School was a wonderful place to me. I never ceased to marvel at all the things there were to learn, and the good part was that each thing I learned seemed to link to something else, and that to something else, and so on and on. It was almost like a constant treasure hunt with the mother lode somewhere near. I didn't know how or if all this information would be useful, but all that mattered was the sheer joy of knowing.

At home, Lizzie and I got along pretty well. I felt protective toward her even though she was almost five years older than I. She embarrassed me because she still talked baby talk a lot even though she could talk as well as anyone when she wanted. I still liked to pick at her a little, usually by teasing her about a boy I knew she didn't like. Some mornings, she would get upset with me about something and start yelling and throwing things at me. I would just leave the house to go to the bus stop. There were as many as ten kids at the bus stop, and they could hear her yelling and fussing at me. Sometimes it was over such trivial stuff that it made no sense. I tried to laugh it off and pretend it didn't matter, but secretly I sometimes wanted to cram a rag in her mouth. She was always arguing with someone on the school bus and making a scene. I usually just let her be unless I thought someone was going to hit her, and then they would hear from me.

I didn't dare invite any of my friends to my house, because if we played games, Lizzie would get mad and insult them if she didn't win every time. She was always falling in and out of love. Most of the time, the guys didn't want to hurt her feelings, but she would shower them with attention to the point of really turning them off. If Dad punished her she would say, "Daddy, don't you wuv wittle wizzy anymore?" She was extreme in her feelings. She either loved a person to death or hated their guts. I knew she needed help, but didn't know what to do for her. It was years later that she was finally treated for her illness.

The summer between my seventh and eighth grade, Lizzie got really sick. She complained that her side hurt, but she was somewhat hypochondriac about feeling ill and enjoyed the special attention she got from dramatizing it to Daddy. One day she started begging me to go get Aunt Veen Webb (Uncle Joe's Wife) to come to our house to see about her. I didn't want to bother Aunt Veen because I thought Lizzie was not really that sick. Finally, I did go, and Aunt Veen came right away. Lizzie was very sick with pneumonia. She came close to dying, and I felt so guilty for not believing her and getting help sooner. Dr. Kelly came every day to see her. He gave her some penicillin shots which had just come out on the market. It was supposed to be the new miracle drug. Dad sat up with her for fourteen days and nights.

I changed her bedding and washed it every day. I remember how hard it was for me to wring the water out of the sheets. I bathed her feverish little body with cool water. It was a hot summer, and we had only a small fan for her. I prayed she wouldn't die. The neighbors began to come around to see if they could help. One young man named John Rainbolt, who worked at Meritts's sawmill with Dad, came and offered to sit up with Lizzie and let Dad get some rest. At first, Lizzie kept calling for Daddy, but the man talked gently to her and got her to calm. The next night, John was back and brought some fruit for Lizzie to eat. He came every other night after that, and Dad got a little rest. Deloyce Cullins, a neighborhood teenager, came and relieved me some during the days. It took forty days before Lizzie was well enough to get up and around.

To my great surprise, I looked up one evening to see a car drive up and stop. It was the school superintendent and his wife! I would not have been more flabbergasted if it had been the President of the United States. They had heard about Lizzie being so sick and had come to see about her. For the first time, I began to see him as the caring person he really was.

CHAPTER 9

Changing Times

Belfast *was an ever changing little cosmos.* People came and went so often that we were always getting new neighbors. Granny Noble moved away and a Cullins family bought her place. That family included Aunt Phronia, Walter, and Bossie her two sons. They were related to the several Cullins families already living in Belfast. Aunt Phronia was in her seventies and her heart was bad. I loved to go by and talk to her as she sat out on her front porch. The house had a front porch that spanned part of the east side next to Busick's store, and it had a "dog run" hallway that ran the length of the house separating two bedrooms from the three other rooms. The "dog run style" was used a lot in buildings because it helped the house stay cooler in the summer. People also had high ceilings to help cool the inside.

Aunt Phronia had raised four children and had lots of grandchildren. One of her grandchildren, Ginger, came to stay with her almost every summer. Ginger and I became almost inseparable. Ginger was so happy-go-lucky that she didn't let Lizzie bother her, so the three of us got along pretty well.

Mrs. Busick had sold the store and moved to Little Rock to be with her daughter, Vada. A family named Willbanks bought the store. Mr. Willbanks financed some of the people who hauled paper wood so he had a thriving business. Mrs. Wilbanks took part in church activities and helped in the store. They had a little daughter named Patricia who was about five years old. The Wilbanks tried to liven up the community by participating in church work and giving a few square dances. The community was too religiously conservative to mesh the two activities. Dancing had been the root of much contention in times past. People had been turned out of the church for even attending a dance. I think it was associated with excessive drinking and lascivious behavior. Religious fevor seemed to swing from one extreme to the other. As far as I could tell, the Wilbanks just encouraged good clean fun with none of the above excesses.

Idus Webb, Uncle Joe's son, married Esta Lee Buie and they started a family in the Crockett Webb house across the track from Joe's store. Idus had a drinking problem, but was good hearted like his dad and was always helping people. Their first four children were Billy, Sissy, Velma Jean, and Honey. They had three more later, but those were the older ones that I knew well.

Mr. Ed Harrington had bought a filling station and grocery store in Sheridan on the corner of Highway 35 and Vine Street, and a Covington family had bought the Harrington place. I didn't see Virginia very much after that. Buck Covington and his wife Ethel had a son everyone called Buddy. He was only about three years old when they moved in. I would go over and push him in his swing and talk to him. He called me his "Lossie Honey." He played mostly with the Webb children. As the kids grew, Billy, Honey, and Buddy would knock down wasps' nests to get the wasp larvae to use for fish bait. Uncle Joe had a huge fish pond on the north end of his property, and it was a dream place to fish.

I enjoyed the kids in my neighborhood, and liked reading to them on Sunday afternoons. They were a ready, willing audience, and I loved to read. I had learned to ride my bicycle quite well, and since none of them had a bicycle, I would ride them all over the place on mine. I had a flat luggage carrier on back and a basket in front. Sometimes I rode two of them in back and one on the handle bars. The road was dirt and sand so the few spills we had did not cause much injury.

Sister Martha had divorced Russell Stancil and had married Roy Aden, who was related to the Cullins families. Roy owned a house located just before the sharp curve as one entered Belfast from the west side. They made a good pair, and I liked visiting with them. Lizzie and I would borrow Martha's electric iron to iron our clothes each week. We only had a flatiron that had to be heated on the stove. Those were always too hot or too cold, or smutty from the smoke. We washed and starched our clothes and hung them on a clothesline to dry. We then sprinkled them down with just a small bit of water and rolled them up for ironing. It was fun and a novelty to get to iron with an electric iron.

Lizzie and I soon were in demand around the neighborhood to help people with their washing. We made a little extra money and could buy personal things we needed. We would help Esta Lee Webb with her laundry almost every week. With all her children, it took almost all day on the rub board with the big bar of P&G soap. (The P&G meant Proctor and Gamble, the manufacturers, but we called it Push and Grunt soap.).

Another lady we washed for was Mrs. Mildred Harrington. She had four boys: Jimmy, Roy, Larry, and Billy Wayne. An infant girl named Jenny Katherine was born while she lived near Belfast. Her husband, J., (son of Mr. Ed Harrington) was in the army in France. She had a difficult time by herself, so her brother, John Rainbolt, came to stay with her and help her with house and yard work and serve as mentor to the kids.

John had a truck and hauled pulpwood. It was strenuous work constantly stretching his long, thin arms and legs taut against his six-foot-six inch frame. He always wore a comical looking striped shop cap that pressed slightly on his large ears making them look like antennae. That cap was a multipurpose tool. It could shade the head and eyes from the sun, be used to wipe profuse sweat, and to swat horse flies, bugs, or mosquitoes that came for a snack. John and that cap were inseparable. When on occasion he allowed it to be washed, it was starched and shaped over a jug to dry. The crisp look of the cap and the thin upright stripes seemed to extend his head upward another six inches and made him look like Jughead in the comic strip.

John's family was from Birdtown, sixteen miles north of Morrilton. His mother died at fifty-two, and his father was so lonely, he remarried within a very short time. His new wife had five children. John's sister, June, was the youngest of the Rainbolt kids and the only one left at home. She was used to having the run of the place. She was so feisty that she was dubbed with the nickname "Cat" which stuck with her as long as she lived. She resented those five new siblings, and ran off from home hoping to get to her brother, John. The police picked her up and brought her back home before she got very far. In a few days she ran off again. That time she reached Belfast where John and Mildred were. John talked to his Dad about letting her stay. He rented an old pharmacy building there in Belfast, got a couple of beds and basic cooking utensils from a used furniture place in Sheridan, and they set up housekeeping. June started to Sheridan School, but she was so far behind in school work that she was embarrassed and soon quit.

I loved June. She was older than I was, but she treated me like a peer. She would show me pictures of her boy friends who were mostly guys in army uniforms. I had the feeling she was somewhat of a dreamer like me. She didn't know as much about cooking as I did because she had never had to cook. One afternoon when I was visiting her, she looked up at the clock and said, "Gracious, it is four-thirty! I had better start some supper for John." She built a fire in the cook stove, washed some dried beans, and put them on to cook. John was to be home by five. I knew those beans would barely be hot by the time he came home. Would he rant and rave? My dad was very strict with us about having a meal ready and on the table when he got home. If we were a few minutes late, he cussed a lot and told us we were no account and lazy.

I cringed for June when John came in. He said, "Sis, is supper ready?" She explained that it would be a while, so he left and went across the tracks to the store. He bought a loaf of bread and some bologna, brought it back and shared with us. He said, "Put those beans in the icebox. We will eat them tomorrow." I couldn't believe my eyes or my ears. I thought "My brother would never have been that kind to me." I remembered how John had helped so much when Lizzie had been sick, and everyone was always saying nice things about him, but it never occurred to me that a guy would be that good to his sister.

I liked to listen to them talk about things that happened when they were kids together. Once, John had tried to build a steam engine from a gas tank. He filled the tank with water and built a big fire under it. It got to steaming pretty good, then blew all to pieces. (John had always loved to tinker with old cars, and even when ten to twelve years old, could interchange parts and assemble some fantastic things.) Another story they told was about a bull. John's dad had made a yoke for it and used it for a plow horse. John liked to ride the bull bareback. On one such occasion, when John was cautiously riding the bull around the yard, June decided she wanted to put her cat up there on the bull's back. The cat got scared and started clawing; the bull reared up and threw John up into the air. He landed on a farm harrow and was knocked cold. June thought he was dead She cried over his limp body and begged him not to die. He came around while she was in her hysteria and opened an eye. She felt embarrassed about making such a fool of herself and was mad at him for scaring her so badly. They laughed and laughed together like life was a big joke.

They were just poor, simple folks like everyone else in Belfast. Somehow I sensed that being poor was not too important if there was love enough to go around. I never felt really secure in my own situation. It seemed like most people I knew would be friendly for a while, but then if I did the least thing to make them offended, they would look for opportunities to recount any of my past misdeeds and air them out to everyone like dirty laundry. There seemed to be no forgetting any misstep no matter how trivial. Instead of settling an issue, they used devious ways to get even. I was not taught the principle of complete forgiveness, but through those two young people, I began to see what a difference it would make if people would just try to get along with each other.

Near the end of World War II, it became a bit easier to get things that had been scarce. Dad managed to get some pretty dress material. Lizzie and I didn't know how to sew and were afraid we would make a mess of trying to make dresses and waste the material. Dad asked June if she would make them and she agreed. She not only got a dress out of my piece, but also a skirt that fit me better than any other skirt I have ever had.

After that June went to Missouri to visit her sister, Lucille, and family. She met a young man by the name of Isbell there, and they got married. They moved to Belfast for a time, and I went to visit her. Her husband seemed so nice. It was summer and dusty. We all went barefooted. Her husband brought a pan of water and washed her feet. Now I thought that was the kind of guy I would like to have, but the marriage lasted only a short time and she came back to John. They rented another house near the Smirl's home. Soon their dad moved in with them with still another new woman they called Mary. This one had a son my age named Benford. He rode our school bus and was well mannered.

I didn't see much of June during that time because she lived a little farther away, but I still loved her like a sister. John and his dad were working in the woods with a fellow named

H. B. Cullins. Everyone called him Bossie. Bossie was a forty-year old bachelor and June was twenty. He had a dry sense of humor and a perky grin. June fell for him, and they were soon married. She moved in next door to me, and that made me happy. In a short time they had a little boy they named Harlan Eugene and called him Gene for short. (I liked that name because Gene Autry was one of my cowboy idols along with Roy Rogers and Dale Evans even though that had nothing to do with his acquiring that name.) June starched and ironed his clothes and kept him so neat and clean that he always looked more like a miniature businessman than a small child. I visited them often and played with Gene. John came by to see her often, and he and June were always full of their usual fun. One day John was telling about their dad driving the log wagon and the horses jerked and pawed when the log wagon got stuck. Mr. Rainbolt, Sr. was not known for patience when he was hot and tired and sweaty. John said his dad cussed at the horses, tore his hat off his head, and began to stomp it. John, thinking to make the situation more ridiculous, said he ran over there and started stomping the hat, too.

Mr. Rainbolt, Sr. stopped and said, "What in the hell are you doing?"

John said, "Helping you stomp your hat!"

The older man saw how ridiculous the matter was and started laughing. John always had a way of turning a potentially flammable situation into a joking matter.

Bossie's mother and brother Walter had welcomed June into their family, and she and Bossie lived in the two rooms of their house separated by the center hall. Aunt Phronia was a kind lady who always read her Bible. I called her Aunt Phronia because it was a custom to use terms of respect and endearment for older people. Aunt Phronia went to church every time the doors opened. She had been widowed for some years but loved to talk about her late husband, Will. She laughed a lot and told me stories about herself when she grew up. Ginger and I spent hours on her porch listening to her reminisce.

Two other ladies that I really liked to be around were Uncle Joe Webb's wife, Veen, and her sister Stella. Aunt Stella had lived alone until she had a stroke, then moved in with Joe and Veen. They were about the only people in the neighborhood that took the daily newspaper, the Arkansas Gazette. I made a habit of running by their house after school and reading the funnies. A friend, Mabel Thompson and I used to read the Katzenjammer Kids and laugh about their antics.

After Aunt Stella's house was emptied, Aunt Laura Cullins and her daughter Rosie Rucker moved into her house. Rosie's husband, Fred Rucker, was there occasionally, but he seemed to come and go.

Many of the older ladies would try to tell us young ones what was the proper roles for ladies. Some of their ideas were quite helpful, but some of them were from the dark ages. One of them said that young girls shouldn't wear bras, but have their blouses loose enough that no one knew what size their breasts were. Proper ladies should wear dresses down to their ankles. To really dress up one needed hat and gloves. At one time, a family with two lovely teenage girls moved into the Crockett Webb house and really caused a flurry by wearing walking shorts to the store. I received a lot of mixed and confusing messages on correct behavior, proper dress and sexual posturing. One lady scolded me for wearing my jeans to church. I had no slip for a dress, and a "lady" did not wear a dress without a slip, and for goodness sake, did not let the slip show around the dress hem. Besides, the church was cold in winter. It was a big hull of a building with a high ceiling and lots of windows that leaked air. It had only one pot-bellied heater that we huddled around on cold days.

Nevertheless, the church was like a beacon in the community. Two staunch deacons guarded the faith, Mr .Avan Busick, the self-appointed janitor and village storekeeper, and Mr. Mac Carder, an elderly man with a face as bearded and white as Moses, and whom I thought must have seen God himself. After those two died, the only ones left to carry on were a few ladies and children. Most of the men gathered in old barns or in the back of Webb's Store to play poker when they were not working. It was almost like church was a sissy thing only for women and children who prayed so their families would be saved and their husbands would not go to hell. People said that, at the time the church was built in the early 1900's, it was packed every meeting day. The only times I remember it being really packed was when there was a funeral or we had homecoming day with all day singing and dinner on the ground or the children gave a Christmas play. I wondered why there had been such "a falling away." It seemed to me that if the story of Christ were true, and I believed it was, then it was worth remembering at times other than Christmas, so I continued to go and felt my courage lifted and my heart lightened.

I wanted so badly to learn to play the piano since we only had two or three ladies in the whole community who could play even a little, but dad could not afford lessons. One lady named Mrs. Henley occasionally tried to show me how to play, but she wanted me to watch her and not touch the piano myself. It was like learning to swim without getting wet. I did want to help wherever I could to show that I loved Jesus, so decided I would help rake leaves and clean the church yard. Once Lizzie and I were really ambitious and decided to scrub the church floor. It had oil on it and Mr. Busick cleaned it with a dust mop. We were used to using the leftover wash water to scrub the floors at home, so I thought it would be a good service to God if we would carry water across our field and give the church floor a good scrubbing. We wanted it to be a wonderful surprise, so we kept it quiet. It took us all day to get all the oil off the floor and make it sparkling clean. We couldn't wait for people to see it. Our pride wilted when people got mad about it, and Mr. Busick said we were pesky kids. He put more oil on it and said for us to let it alone.

Summer revivals were fun. Usually it was hot and the bugs swarmed into the church fluttering around the Aladdin lamps while we sat back on the pews and fanned ourselves with cardboard fans that were furnished by the Buie Funeral Home. Brother Homer Laster preached one revival. He was bald headed, and a huge bug kept landing on his head as he pounded the pulpit. It didn't look much like the dove that lighted on Jesus, but sure did put him in the Spirit! Ladies took turns fixing supper for the preacher during the revival, and you could tell the excess fried chicken usually made him a bit short winded. There was always a glass of cool water on the pulpit for him to moisten his mouth so he could get a second wind.

The singing schools were fun, too. They usually ran every night for a week or two. We did the "Do Re Mi Fa So La Ti Do" up the scale and back down to tune our voices. The notes were shaped, and we tried to read them when they were all mixed up on the music sheets. We used the Stamps-Baxter book for a text. Charles Carr, one of our teachers, was a writer of hymns and knew a lot about music. My sister, Martha, liked to sing in the "choir." She had absolutely no sense of timing and was always way ahead or behind everyone else. To beat the timing, she had no sense of volume either, so could drown everyone else out. The preacher, Joe Poe at that time, felt he should speak to her and get her to tone it down a bit. As we all thought, his good intentions led the way to hell. She was so offended that she said she would never come back. Joe was so sorry to have offended her that he went to her house and begged her pardon on bended knee. She forgave him and resumed the status quo. I am very sure she is singing in that heavenly chorus today and that the Lord has blessed her with a lovely voice.

Martha had a little boy she named Paul because she admired the Apostle Paul. As soon as Paul could get around, he waddled up to the pulpit and helped the preacher preach by jabbering and waving his arms. Martha made such a commotion trying to retrieve him that it would probably have been better to let him be. She would say, "You betta git down from der, Paul boy." All the while she would be rushing up to yank him down and he would be laughing and trying to run from her. Poor Baby Paul! I knew how tough it was on him. By that time I could see that Martha usually meant well, but didn't realize a lot of things. She would try to save money by cutting Paul's hair herself. It lay in uneven ridges and gullies all across his head. Paul never lost his desire to preach even though he couldn't talk very plain. He preached on the radio from Benton for a long time, and several people professed Christ because of him.

Roy and Martha always tried to make a garden of sorts, and Martha canned what she could. She could piece quilts and made beautiful designs. Houses were so drafty that people slept with several quilts on top of them in the winter. Roy worked hard at a sawmill, but was illiterate and had few marketable skills so they were always very poor. I went by their house and saw them eating just popcorn for meals many times. Sometimes they made what they called "fish gravy." It consisted of browned cornmeal in grease and they would sop it with biscuits.

Martha began to read her Bible quite a bit although she didn't understand it very well. She read the part where it says, "Thou shalt not commit adultery" and began to worry so much because she had been married before that she divorced her husband Roy and went to live with a Pentecostal couple. Since she had minimum work experience, she found it hard to make a living for her and Paul. After about a year, she and Roy remarried. When Paul was nine years old, Martha became ill with cancer and died. I was really sad at her funeral because I felt that she had never really lived in the sense of having much enjoyment. Roy was despondent and started wearing her clothes. No one could believe their eyes to see Roy out chopping wood in a dress. It was especially unusual in Belfast because the men prided themselves on their "manhood", especially if it came to washing dishes or doing "woman's work." Roy even started buying women's underwear a few years before he died.

The Pentecostal couple that had influenced Martha to leave Roy lived in the house just up the hill from them. They were evidently missing a few marbles themselves because they didn't act like any of the nice Pentecostals I had known at school. The woman probably weighed about five hundred pounds, and the two would go to town in their pick-up truck with her riding in back on a board laid across the bed next to the cab. She couldn't fit into the cab. He would just drive along while the wind whipped her hair and dress tail. They would whoop and holler at everyone they saw on the way to town and shout "Whooee Jesus" like they were calling the razorback hogs.

One day Dad found out that they had gone to Benton and checked Mom out of the asylum and were keeping her at their house. She had gotten so much worse through the years that she didn't realize what it was all about. The man claimed he was going to heal Momma. Dad was so infuriated that he thought about killing the man, but changed his mind and went for the sheriff. By the time the sheriff got there, the fellow had taken Mom back to the hospital. Dad and the sheriff gave him a strong verbal warning to let Belle alone. As one could see, Belfast had its good neighbors and enough kooks to keep life interesting and people stirred up.

I had ambitions of being a cartoon artist when I was about thirteen. Dad let me order a correspondence course from the Cartoonist Exchange. It had about twenty-four lessons. I got a little gummy-like statue of a stick man about ten inches high with the course. I could bend it in different shapes and use it as a model to draw. The neighbor kids would come, and I would show them my drawings. It encouraged me that they seemed to like them. One day while Lizzie and I were at school, a couple of five-year-old girls came to our house, lifted the latch and walked in. They scattered all my art work, broke a spare eye I had in a small red patent-leather purse, then went to the kitchen and poured out flour, coffee, sugar, salt, and lots of other things in the floor. Then they broke about a dozen eggs on top of all that. We knew who did it because their little foot and hand prints were everywhere and one of them left her jump rope in the yard. I was despondent that they would do that and wondered what I had done to them that would make them want to do such a thing. The little girls denied doing it, but one of the dads came down and saw the mess and believed his little girl had helped do it, and she got a spanking. I didn't realize then that five-year-olds just act on impulse without thinking or knowing about consequences.

Fifty years later one of the little girls, now grown, looked me up to apologize for that incident. She said it had nagged her and made her feel guilty all her life. I was sorry it had caused her such pain. We had a nice visit, and I was glad they had not done it out of revenge for some supposed wrong I had done them. She told me I had been an inspiration to her with my simple art work and she had gone on to become an art teacher. I got to see her mother, Mildred again and met her husband, Ronald, who shared my love for poetry.

The two summers after my seventh and eighth grade years Dad let the community use our field for a baseball diamond, and Belfast teemed with excitement for this traditional all-American game. There were enough young men for a good team and lots of adults to cheer them on. The guys would practice hard during the week for games with other small community teams on Saturdays. A few of us girls practiced with the boys on weekday afternoons. We played softball in PE class at school, and it was a good excuse to hone our skills at flirting. It seemed that everybody in Belfast turned out for the Saturday games, and people came for miles around to see the games. One entrepreneur thought to set up a business on the back of his pick up truck. He had tubs of iced cokes and boxes of Babe Ruth, Butterfinger, Hersheys and other candy snacks to sell. That was one of those ideas that I envied because I didn't think of it myself. (No matter, I would not have had the resources to finance it).

Martha never missed a game, and she was really gung-ho with her enthusiasm. People watched her more than they watched the games. She jumped and hollered and heckled the opposing players and umpire until she would have put some of the most seasoned Razorback cheerleaders to shame. She would get so steamed up that it wouldn't be long until she would make a bee line for the privy on the edge of the field behind our house. She would make short work of her necessary business, and pop right back out to keep from missing a single play. She was oblivious to anyone or anything around her in the heat of her excitement.

Hensley was our biggest competitor. Bossie and Walter had an old stripped-down flat bed truck, and they would load up fifteen or twenty people and go to the games when the games were away. Martha never failed to hitch a ride. It wouldn't have been the same without her.

Another favorite pastime was washers. People would gather around the porch at Busick's store and compete in washer games. The game was laid out with five Vienna sausage cans buried to the rim in the ground, four forming the corners of a square and one in the center like the dots on number five dominoes. The playing pieces were large metal washers. A player standing behind a line about 10 to 15 feet away would throw the washers one at a time. If one landed in a can, the player scored points depending on which hole they hit. The center can counted a whopping five points. Other holes counted one to four around the outer edge. If the first player scored, the second player would try to "kill" his points by having a washer land on top of any that made a hole. (Similar to horse shoe ringers) The first person to score 21 was the winner, but if he accidentally scored over 21, he went "bust" and had to start over. The winner challenged anyone in the crowd to play against him. Sometimes the game was so popular that two playing units were used and four players could play either singly or as partners. Someone improvised a homemade wooden scoreboard with sliding numbers and letters. The "Champion" issued his challenge with a lot of fanfare and jesting as the scoreboard was pulled out and readied for each event. We kids set up our own washer game in our yard, and I practiced until I was a pretty adept player. It was a fun game that included all ages and required no expensive equipment or large stadium. I liked the simplicity.

When I got to the ninth grade, our group thought we were superettes. I took home economics and learned to cook and sew a bit more. Our teacher was the lovely Miss Elizabeth Holmes (Lancaster). She taught us to cook from a recipe using exact measurements. I had cooked all my life, but it was mainly dab/dash cooking...a dab of this or a dash of that. Now I learned to do it the "right" way. Even though most recipes called for ingredients I had never heard of, I learned to substitute a lot of things that sometimes worked. The gas and electric cook stoves at school were no match for the wood burning stove I had gotten used to at home. I could already make cornbread and fried potatoes that rivaled the local "chef's". My main rule of cooking had been; if I make a mess, throw it to the hogs and try again. The hogs got pretty fat, too.

My dad had bought me an old treadle Singer sewing machine. It was so old the thread had worn a groove in the metal plate as it fed from the spool to the needle. The bobbin was elongated, and I only had a single one, so I had to unwind remaining thread before I could change colors. It had no back-tack, so all the threads had to be tied at the end of the seam. When I started sewing on the electric machines at school, they had knee controls. They would zoom up a seam faster than I could get started on mine at home. Once when I was sewing in Home Ec. Class, the machine was going so fast, I couldn't guide the material. I forgot to take my knee off the control, and in my excitement to slow it down, I made it go faster. I yelled, "Whoa, Whoaaaa!" as loud as I could. Everyone was teary-eyed from laughing at me. I finally moved my knee, and that machine stopped. Some of the girls kept ha-hawing and asked me if I thought I was plowing Old Maud.

I wasn't the only one who had problems. Jo Ann Beck, one of our very smartest and nicest girls, was making a dress. She came to me with tears in her eyes one day and asked me to look at her project. She knew it didn't look right, but couldn't figure out what was wrong. I looked it over and suppressed my urge to laugh. She had sewed a sleeve in the neck hole of her dress.

Later, when I started to make a sun dress with a bolero top, I was so overconfident that I made another goof. Miss Holmes showed us how to cut and fit our pattern. She let us choose our own pattern. She told me that the one I chose was difficult, but she thought I could do it. That was a challenge. I could already sew pretty well except for the awful buttonholes, but this one only had a zipper along the side. The teacher cautioned us to take our material home and wet it good then iron it to get the shrinkage out of it before we cut. I decided that mine was going to take longer to make, and I might not have time to finish. She wouldn't know if I didn't shrink it first. I just laid the pattern out and cut. The dress turned out beautifully and I was so proud of it along with the "A" I made for making it. Some time later, however, when I washed it, the skirt, cut on the bias to make a circle, shrunk on only one side. It never looked good again. I made sure Miss Holmes didn't know about that.

Two years of home economics taught me a lot of things I needed to know. It was hard to relate some of the things to my home life, though. For instance, we were taught to set a table with a tablecloth, cloth napkins, water goblets, polished silverware, centerpiece...the whole bit. There was certainly no way to practice that at home with the mismatched plates from oatmeal premiums, cracked cups, and snuff glasses. It seemed like two worlds.

I learned to love basketball and took part in an intramural program where the classes competed. Sometimes the girls played against the boys; sometimes girls played against girls. During one game, I chased the ball that was going out of bounds. Another girl and I bumped heads so hard, I could feel my glass eye crack. She fell flat and went off the court complaining that her head hurt. I finished the game and said nothing about the eye. I was worried. That night my fears were realized when I removed the eye to wash it. It came apart in my hand. I didn't know what to do. There was no way I could get another eye before school tomorrow. I had not missed a day in three years, but didn't want to go with an eye missing. I decided to bandage it and go on to school. By the end of the day, I was exasperated with everyone asking me what was wrong with my eye. This seemed so much worse than when I was six. I was a teenager now. Looking good was more of a priority. I had long hair so I thought about pulling it over to hide half of my face and keeping my head down. I felt so hideous.

In a matter of weeks, Dad took me to Little Rock to try to get a new eye. We went to the Donaghey Building where there was a clinic. They had drawer after drawer of ready made plastic eyes…blue, brown, every color imaginable for eyes. The man first tried to match my color which is a strange mix of blue, brown, and green. When he got a near color match, he began to try them in my socket. Some were too big, some too little, some looked up, some looked down or sideways…gosh, what a bummer! Finally, they settled on one that was too large, but held the lid open. When I moved the eye, it turned up slightly. I grew despondent and self-conscious over the eye. For the first time, I was really glad when school was out.

The fun of the school bus ride had deteriorated over the years. It seemed that there was always an older student bully picking on the younger kids by yanking off their caps, throwing their books out the window, pulling their hair, and keeping them almost in tears all the way home. Some of the younger ones liked to pick at Lizzie because she was a ready target with her hot temper. I cringed at what I interpreted as an explosive setting. Student government was supposed to be operative on the school buses just as it was in the study hall at school. High school boys were employed to drive the buses to save the district money. These young men were carefully chosen, and for the most part, did a good job. They were versed in traffic safety issues. A red flag bearer exited the bus in front of students at each stop and conducted them safely across the road. When traffic built up behind the bus because of frequent stops, the driver would find a safe place to pull over and let the traffic by. However, the driver had no authority over his cargo other than to report any misbehavior to the administration. He could not fully concentrate on his driving and keep his eye peeled at the rearview mirror. Hauling children was much like hauling cattle; the load shifted as they moved about with no seat belt protection. Some wandered the aisles obviously looking for mischief. The threat of retaliation kept most everyone from reporting an incident. Frequently an ill-informed mother would board the bus and "bless" everyone out for something her child had allegedly suffered at the hand of some other student. More often than not, her chastisement only worsened the situation for her child as he/she became more the object of ridicule as a "momma's baby".

One especially chaotic situation arose on my bus one afternoon when two boys were scuffling on the bus. A boy standing in the aisle while the bus was moving grabbed a head lock on a boy that was seated. With a smile of reluctant tolerance, the one seated reached back and pulled him over his shoulder. The student standing, lost his balance as the bus jarred from a road bump. His head hurled forward and hit the iron support on the back of a seat. He grew livid with anger and came up fighting for real. He drew out a jack knife to threaten the other student. Almost every boy carried a pocket knife as a staple. Usually the blade was about three inches long and used to clean and trim fingernails, and toenails, cut strings, whittle, or other useful purposes. This knife had a blade long enough to skin a deer. The angry guy hit the other one in the nose again and again until his opponent's face was a bloody mess. When the opponent tried to return the blows, the knife wielder would wave the knife in his face. This continued until the bloodied student got to his place to exit the bus. He had to back out of the bus with the knife in his face. The driver tried to stop the fight, but was threatened also. Finally, the boy with the knife got back on the bus, sat down, and put away his knife.

Everyone was silent as death. We all wondered if anyone would report the incident, and. if not, would the next one prove deadly. The next morning, Lizzie made a bee line to Mr. McKenzie's office to report the happenings. I had no idea she was going to do that until we boarded the bus that afternoon. Lizzie was sitting near the front, and I was about four seats back. The boy got on the bus and immediately began to harangue her about reporting him and getting him in trouble. She smarted back at him and the argument began. I knew she would not back down if he cut her to pieces. He got loud; she got louder. He soon asked her if she wanted him to slap her. When he said that, I got between them and told him he would have to slap me first. He looked surprised and asked, "Who pulled your chain?"

I told him that Lizzie had been the only person with courage enough to stand up for what was right, and that I was ashamed

I had not gone with her. He could easily have brushed me roughly aside, but was so surprised that I spoke up, that, for the first time, he was at a loss for words. He went to the back of the bus and sat down mumbling to himself. I was trembling inside. After that incident and a few similar ones, the yellow bus lost most of its charm for me.

Lizzie graduated that year. Her class was the 49ers; their symbol was the covered wagon, reminiscent of the Gold Rush to California in 1849. Her classmates had been like guardian angels to her through the years. Sarah Wilkerson and Mary Lou Wynne had been especially kind. Lizzie's favorite teacher was Mrs. Nall, and, through the years, she never failed to remember Mrs. Nall with a Christmas card. Not much attempt was made to help her secure vocational training, so dad let her order a correspondence business course which she worked on sporadically until she finally gave up.

I entered tenth grade in the fall of 1949. Things went well the first four months. I still struggled with my self image, but was determined to not let it get me down. Somewhere I stumbled across the Serenity Prayer and it inspired me to turn my attention to better things than my own physical misshape. I drew a lot of inspiration from different writers. Most of the stories at that time had a stated moral unlike the more modern trend of leaving a person to figure out the lesson for himself. Of course people were beginning to ask me what I was going to do when I graduated. I had no idea what I could do. I had no network of support. As far as I knew, no scholarships were available. School counseling was just beginning to take hold, but just consisted of the counselor testing and calling a student in for a ten-minute conference once a year. Everyone was required to take a new course called "Occupations" which mainly was a survey of different jobs and skills they required. Few of those jobs focused on women. Women were expected to be housewives, nurses, teachers, or waitresses. How could I make money which was so necessary to raising my station in life? For men, the world was their oyster.

In January, Dad announced to us that Ellen was coming home to stay. She had become such a problem to Aunt Cora that auntie decided she might be better off with her dad. They lived in the rural area of Corinth community, and Ellen was bad about wandering off to neighbor's houses two or three miles away. Auntie would be so worried until she was finally found. Ellen was eleven years old and beginning to show signs of physical development. She was very self-conscious about her protruding front teeth. Kids had begun to call her "Bugs Bunny" or horse. She did not take to teasing well and would regularly hit people. Even when a person was just joking and laughing with her, she would start a nudging, slapping routine that got harder and harder. I had thought she was just unsure of herself because of the sudden change in her life. She talked about Aunt Cora constantly, calling her mom. She thought everything we did was not as "mom" did. Indeed, it probably wasn't. She was to graduate sixth grade that spring, and Dad asked me to make her a graduation dress. She said she didn't want me to make it that Mom would. I would have been relieved to not have the responsibility, but Dad said we didn't want to bother Auntie, and for me to go ahead and make it. I let her choose her pattern and material and did the best I could.

She and Lizzie didn't hit it off from day one. Dad was patronizing to Ellen because he had not got to spend much time with her when she was little. Lizzie was fiercely jealous and showed it relentlessly in so many ways. One day I looked out the window and Lizzie and she were up the road a ways and Lizzie was whipping Ellen. I hurried out to stop her and find out what the matter was. Lizzie said Ellen had been picking Mother's roses. Mother had planted a seven-sister cluster rose in the corner of the yard of our old house. The rose bush had not been cared for, and had spread out through the years to cross the road and come forth on the railroad right-of-way. Ellen had admired the roses and cut a few intending to bring them to the house. There were thousands of blooms out there, but Lizzie determined that Ellen should not have cut any of them because they belonged to our mother. She was always telling Ellen she was not her sister. I became the referee, forever trying to keep those two from tangling.

As spring turned into warmer weather, we three girls were crowded in the one bed we shared. The mattress was made of cotton sacks sewed together and the loose cotton inside had to be reshuffled every day to make it as nearly even as we could get it. Each of my sisters insisted on sleeping next to me, so I was stuck in the middle with both of them rolling down and stifling me. One night in early June, I was so sweaty and uncomfortable that I could not get to sleep. I lay there and waited until I thought they were both asleep, then I quietly slipped out, pulled a quilt off the shelf, and lay down on a makeshift pallet in the floor. Soon Lizzie roused and missed me. Here she came. No sooner had she got settled than Ellen woke and moved down, too. We were like three pigs rooting for a comfort zone. I was cross with both of them, and we got into an argument. Dad, whose bed was in the same room, woke up as we were wrangling. He got out of bed, got his belt, and started to whip me. The other two had popped into bed again and were under the covers. I had no explanation, no solution. The whipping somehow made me feel better. I hoped it did my Dad. I could not cry.

Ginger came back to stay a month with Aunt Phronia a day or two later. I was so glad to see her. She was the one giggly friend I could count on. Ginger was now fourteen and had grown tall. She was a pretty young woman. I was sixteen, but short. We were together every day when I could get away from the sisters. They would usually visit Martha during the day. Ginger and I spent a lot of time with June. John was staying with June and Bossie at the time. They lived in the Wilbanks' house where the Busick's used to live. The Wilbanks' had moved to Conway. Ginger wanted to see what it was like to have a boy friend, so she persuaded John to set her up with his friend, Bobby Joe . We four would sit on the porch of Busick's store in the evenings and just talk. Bobby Joe had not had many girl friends so he was really shy. John was a good talker and could keep the conversation going. He was a sort of chaperone for Ginger.

One day Ginger asked me if I liked John. I told her I thought he was one of the nicest people I had ever seen, but he was twenty-six. She told me he liked me, but I thought it was just a friendship thing. June had an ice cream supper later that week, and we made ice cream with an old time crank freezer. We all laughed and cut up a little. and I thought it would be funny to put ice down John's shirt. He was bent over the freezer and I slipped up behind him and dropped it behind his collar. He jumped up and grabbed at me. We both laughed as he shook the ice out. One night the Lucas family had a play party. Ellen wanted to go, so John and I walked her to the gate and then went back and climbed upon a stack of crossties near the track where we had a panoramic view of the party. We watched for a while then went and sat on the porch at the store. Bobby Joe and Ginger came and sat with us. By this time they were pretty serious about each other. Ginger was to leave for her home in Texas the next day, and they were both sad that they were to be parted.

Ginger's brother drove a big truck, and he was to come by and pick her up. She invited me to go down to Daingerfield, Texas with them and visit her for a few days. She said her brother would be coming back through and would bring me back home. She asked my dad, and he said OK. I was toying with the idea of going. I thought it might be nice to get away from the girls a few days. Maybe I could figure some good ways to help them get along better. We played cards at June's that night, and John insisted on walking me home. He said he wanted to talk to me. He asked me if I was going home with Ginger, and I told him I hadn't decided. He said he didn't want to tell me what to do, but her brother drank a little much sometimes. He implied that I might not be safe.

It was nice to know someone cared about my safety, but I didn't really think there was danger. Anyway, I thanked John for his concern. We talked about school and the bus ride. He was so easy to talk to. He then asked me if I would marry him. He said he would not promise to be good to me, but would treat me so many ways I would have to like some of them. I was sure he would be better to me than anyone had ever been. I thought it would be nice to have someone all my own who cared and would love me for myself. Could I accept and return the love that he so freely offered? I really didn't know, but it was worth a try. It never occurred to me how we would make a living, but the important thing I wanted was someone to care.

As was the custom, John asked my dad the next day about our getting married. Dad agreed. His one request was that John take me to see my mother from time to time. It touched me that Dad sometimes gave a little glimpse into his deep feelings for Mom when I least expected it. John applied for a marriage license then made a trip to Birdtown where he borrowed $65 to use to get married. On July 6, 1950, a strange caravan of people consisting of John, myself, Dad, Martha, Lizzie, Ellen, June and several others headed for Benton where John and I were married in the court house there by a Mr. Hunnicutt who was a justice of the peace. There was no organ playing, no beautiful bride's maids, no best man, no flowers. It didn't matter.

John & Lossie

We all returned to Belfast after the ceremony, and June prepared fried chicken and lemon pie for our "wedding reception." John had planned for me and him to take the train back to Benton as it came through in the late afternoon. He had changed clothes when we got back and left his billfold in his dress pants. We heard the train coming and went out and boarded the red caboose. The train switched a bit and was about ready to leave when John discovered his billfold was gone. He jumped off the train and ran back to the house shouting to the conductor to wait for him. The conductor said rather grouchily, "We can't do that!" I sat there wondering if I should get off. The conductor asked me if we were just married and I told him we were. He called to the brakeman, "Wait for him, Charlie, but start it moving slow!" Charlie waved his lantern as a signal to the engineer to get the train moving. The engineer started the train up very slowly as the crew laughed at John stretching his long legs running to catch the train. When we arrived at Benton, we walked across town to a cheap motel. It was a very hot day and we were sweaty and dirty. We went into the room and showered. There was no air conditioning. The room was so hot that we raised the windows and decided to walk uptown to the theater and watch a movie until it got cooler. We sat and held hands and ate gobs of popcorn and drank soda pop. We had no idea that that short train ride was the beginning of a fifty year journey together.

Chapter 10

Life's Blooming

The breeze through the open window woke me. It was strange to see a man, lean and strong in the bed beside me. John and I had married just yesterday. We had spent the night in a little motel on Military Road in Benton. It seemed like a dream as I studied the lines of his sleeping face and touched his tousled hair. John was so kind, but I wondered if I was really a woman and ready for all this. This was July, and I would be seventeen in September. John was 26, a good worker, but illiterate. Our romantic dreams were all we had. I slipped out of bed, dressed quickly, and unbolted the door, thinking to go sit outside and clear my head. John sat upright in bed as the bolt made a slight noise.

"Where are you going?" he asked somewhat puzzled.

"No place special, just outside" I answered.

"That's a relief! I was afraid you might be running away," he remarked in a half-serious tone.

"What would you do if I did?" I teased.

"I would run away with you. I can't have my best half on the loose!"

We both laughed as he jumped out of bed and began to get dressed. This was Friday. We had to find an apartment TODAY! John had to go to work Monday and we must be settled in by then. We looked a bit rumpled as we set out walking all over Benton to find a place to live. John's number 12 shoes and long legs gave him the advantage as we walked. He was six foot six, and I was only five foot two with short legs. I had to take two steps to his one in order to keep up. When he was standing with arm outstretched, I fit nicely right under his arm. He was a gentle, sweet, skinny giant. We held hands, and he just sort of kept me in tow. As we walked along, the sun rose higher and the July 7th promised to be a scorcher. We stopped at Hick's grocery on Edison Avenue for a soda. Mr. Hicks, who was dubbed "Hickey" by his friends and customers, was a personal friend to John. The store was not too busy at the time so he took a few minutes to talk to us and congratulate us on getting married. At the same time, he gave a knowing look and made a few joking inferences which turned my face red.

Hickey advised John to see a man named Larry Rose who was a junk dealer that seemed to own half of Benton. Larry had quite a few "low rent" apartments. We left, and located Larry just up the street and asked him about an apartment. He said he didn't have anything at the time, but would fix up something for us in about a week. He referred us to a "Miss Arkie" who had an apartment house northwest of town near where the Saline Memorial Hospital would later be built. We went to see Miss Arkie. She lived alone on half of the lower floor of a two story house. A family of three was renting the other side of the ground floor. Flashing a broad smile, she met us at the door. She was short, had wispy gray hair, and wore a blue chenille robe. Shuffling around in slippers, she led us up stairs to an attic apartment. As we ascended the stairs, I heard what sounded like paper rustling. I look at her as we reached the landing and notice the corner of a sheet of newspaper sticking out the neck of her undershirt. She had her whole bosom stuffed with newspapers. (I never knew for what reason.)

The apartment was spacious considering what we had been used to. It had a kitchen and large bedroom which we could also use as a sitting room. The doorways were only six foot high, so John had to remember to duck before entering or leaving. Since it was an attic room, the walls slanted with the roof as the ceiling slanted downward. John must remember to walk near the high side. Little window alcoves jutted out onto the roof, giving ample light and occasional breeze. A bed, gas cook stove with spider legs, table and chairs, and ice box were furnished. Miss Arkie warned me to keep the melt pan under the ice box emptied because if it ran over it would leak down into her closet below. I made a mental note. We next went back downstairs where she showed us the bathroom. There was one bathroom in the whole house and it downstairs and had to be accessed through Miss Arkie's personal apartment. The one good attribute of the whole house was that it was meticulously clean. John paid the $5.00 required for a week's rent and we left, hoping to return with a few necessities to set up housekeeping.

We hitched a ride on the mail truck going back to Belfast. Several members of both our families shared their meager housekeeping things with us. Lizzie gave me a small skillet; Martha gave a set of plates she had gotten as Quaker Oatmeal premiums; June gave me a few wash cloths and towels saved from buying a certain brand of washing powder; Aunt Phronia gave me a couple of sheets and two old pillows with pillowcases; Dad was generous with the snuff glasses. Everyone contributed what they could to this impromptu "wedding shower". Saturday, we borrowed a few other essentials including a slop jar for a makeshift potty and wash tub for bathing. June and Bossie were kind enough to drive us back to Benton to set up our living quarters. It didn't take long to put our few items in place. The apartment was extremely hot in the afternoon, so as soon as we finished, we went downstairs.

John had told me to make out a list of things I needed, and he would take the list to Hickey's store and get the things on the credit until payday. I had torn off a piece of a calendar and made my list on the back. I had about fifteen items that I needed besides bread, lunch meat and some groceries to do for the week. I folded the list and gave it to John. When he got to the store and handed the list to Hickey, he burst out laughing. John was puzzled about why Hickey was laughing until he showed John the back side of the list. It was a picture of the inside haunches of a large dog. I had not noticed, but Hickey teased me about that every time I entered the store. Just the word "dog" would send him into hysterical laughter. I tried to be a good sport, but dreaded going in the store. I got my chance to get him back soon. One day when I went in, Hickey had gotten some new false teeth. He was trying to get used to them, but they kept whistling as he talked and causing him obvious discomfort. Finally he opened his mouth wide to laugh, and those teeth went flying across the whole store. His face turned red, and I laughed out loud. We agreed that if he shut up about the dog, I wouldn't mention the teeth.

Monday morning John left at 5 a.m. to catch a work truck to the woods where he was to cut logs for a sawmill. I got him off to work with an 8 lb. lard bucket full of biscuits, bacon, and other goodies for lunch. Instead of going back to bed, I began to clean the apartment. That didn't take long so I lay down across the bed to rest a bit. I must have dozed off when I heard a frantic knock at the door. It was Miss Arkie. I had forgotten to empty the melt pan under the ice box and it was overflowing. She had noticed it drenching her closet. I hurriedly emptied the pan and ran downstairs to see what damage was done. Sure enough! There were long wet streaks on the ceiling and down the wallpaper on the closet.

I talked to Miss Arkie after she calmed down. The two of us took a walk in her back yard where I noticed an apple tree loaded with apples. I asked her why she didn't pick them, and she said she couldn't climb up there. I shimmied up the tree and came down with my shirt tail filled with apples. I showed her how to make fried apple pies. She said she hadn't had those since her mother died some years ago. We quickly made friends and she found lots of chores for me to do the following week.

John came home sick that evening. He was shaking and had a high fever. I went down and borrowed some aspirins from Miss Arkie. In an hour or so he sweated it off and dozed off to sleep. He got up about half asleep during the night and cracked his head on the sloped ceiling alcove. That woke him up. I tried to get him to stay home the next day, but he felt he had to work. He had entrusted me with all the money he had…three silver dollars and some change. I kept those for years until they were finally spent for a very special reason.

Late in the week, Larry Rose came over and told us he had an apartment ready for us. He had boxed in the back of an old car repair shop on Edison Avenue and made a single room that was about 20x20. He had sealed the side next to the shop and the overhead with various sizes of boards salvaged from crates he had collected in his junk business. Natural acoustics gave us a complete surround sound. The building had two apartments above. The walls were so porous that we could hear every sound from the apartment directly above. At least we were on a ground floor albeit overlooking an overgrown, rat infested junk yard and a dilapidated old winery cellar.

Miss Arkie chided Larry Rose as he helped us carry our things out. She said, "Larry, why are you stealing away my good tenants?"

"NOT to fuss at me, Miss Arkie," he retorted. "I sent them over here, and you didn't give me a cut for that!"

The wrangling was good-natured. They had known each other for years.

The new apartment had one double window that gave us a good view of a junk yard. There was literally a sea of rusted, dilapidated vehicles out there that were in all stages of disrepair. To the left, what was once a double garage spilled its contents of old magazines, newspapers, and comic books out the drooping, half opened doors onto the trail that led to the outdoor privy and an overflowing trash barrel near a fence overgrown with honeysuckle and blackberry brambles. Beyond the sagging fence was a gray rise with railroad tracks on top of it. I liked the clean slate-and-cinder look of the track bed, and there was a double set of rails leading both ways as far as eye could see. I felt right at home near the track which constantly reminded me of my dreams of far away places and my childhood home. I often stood in the window or doorway and counted the number of cars attached to the big engines. Usually more than a hundred flatcars, boxcars, and tank cars rumbled past before I could see the red caboose. Hundreds of railroad companies shipped goods all over the United States. Trains came thundering through day and night blowing loud blasts as warning for the nearby crossing. One night John was sound asleep when a train rumbled through with an extra heavy load shaking the whole area around us. In his half-dazed state, John thought a tornado was coming. He jumped up, dragged me out of bed by one arm, and was pulling me toward the door. I struggled to get on my feet while frantically trying to get him awake. Finally, he woke enough to turn me loose; then with a puzzled expression, lay back down on the bed and went to sleep again. Eventually we both got used to the noise and shut it out.

I have often thought how necessary it is in life to look beyond the unsightly surroundings and ignore the noises that rudely jar us from reverie to find the beauty and adventure beyond. With that thought in mind, I busied myself in the apartment trying to use what I had to make it look cozy and lived in. I ripped an old sheet and made curtains which I embroidered with bright butterflies. We had gathered up a few more things…an iron bedstead with coil springs, an old mattress, a faded studio couch that served as a couch in the daytime, but would convert into a single bed for guests at night, a huge, ragged overstuffed chair, and a table with 2 wooden nail kegs for chairs. Our landlord Larry Rose brought me some plants from his greenhouse which I set around the room for pretty color and blooms. We cleaned the deep, metal sink which had been used to wash car parts and converted it for kitchen use. At least we had running water! I was happy. I could clean the whole apartment in a half hour with time to spare.

A couple of days after we moved in, I was surprised by a visitor. A pretty young woman who lived in the front upstairs apartment came and knocked on my door. She said, "I am your neighbor, Hazel Davis. I thought I would come by and welcome you." With that she extended her hand which held a big, red tomato. I thanked her and was delighted. She had brought a tomato for herself, so we sat and talked as we ate them. After that Hazel and I were together every day. Hazel's grandmother lived about two blocks up the street. She was 86 years old and still lived alone, did her own washing on a rub board, and always had homemade treats for us when we came by. We both loved to hear her tell stories about her childhood. Hazel gave a Stanley party and invited me to come. I met several more ladies at the party. One of them was Mrs. Inez Shelton who lived in the neat little white house just past the old winery. When Inez found out that John's mother had been Claudia Wright from Birdtown, she figured out that she was a relative of his. She was really into genealogy and gave me a chart with several generations of Wrights and Rainbolts. I had never thought much about genealogy until then, but wished that I knew more about those people of posterity. I wanted to know the joys, frustrations, sweat, and tears they had experienced in their daily lives.

On December 1, 1950, just five months after we were married, we received word that John's dad had been shot. That was a total shock to us. I had never known anyone that was actually murdered and thought that only happened in the movies. We went to stay with Louise, John's sister who lived on Tucker Mountain, for a few days to find out what happened and help with funeral arrangements. The man who shot Mr. Rainbolt was a neighbor named Ray Nichols, a veteran who had been wounded in battle and had a steel plate in his head. They were good friends who got their respective monthly checks that day and went together to get some booze. Rainbolt's wife, Mary, rode along with them. At first, they laughed and had a great time, but as the drinking continued, the relationship began to turn sour. They began to argue over trivial things. From later court testimony, accusations flew as they gradually lost their perspective on reality. By late evening, the altercation had continued to heat up to the point that each was swearing and making threats toward the other. The man went back to his house and got his gun. He stood out in the road in front of the Rainbolt home and shot through the open doorway. Mr. Rainbolt was sitting on his bed and the bullet went through his chest. The neighbor was given a prison term of five years. The family did not have much contact with Mary Rainbolt after Mr. Rainbolt's death. I was sorry all that had happened, and especially sad that I would not get to enjoy John's father and step-mother through the years. Mary was a congenial person, fun to be around and easy to talk to. I had hoped to adopt her as my mother before all that took place.

After the funeral we went back to our apartment at Benton. The weather had turned cold while we were gone and water pipes had burst saturating our whole apartment. Our mattress, clothes, couch, and other belongings were completely soaked. It took days to get everything dried out and life back to somewhat normal. Probably having to do that brought a needed diversion from the horror of the events the week before.

Our first Christmas was only three weeks away from Mr. Rainbolt's untimely death. John got a ninety-five dollar bonus from the Farm Bureau mill where he worked. He wanted me to have a coat. I had not had a new coat since I was nine years old. I wanted to save part of the money because I knew from my Dad's experience with timber work that lay-offs would inevitably come when the weather got really bad. John would not hear of that. He bought me a lovely new coat and a new dress. He could not do very much, but wanted to express his love by sacrificing as much as he could for me. Actually he needed shoes and pants much more than I needed things because he was out in the cold all day while I was in a warm place.

We did have a hard winter and money really was scarce. John and I went rabbit hunting on Owosso Hill during a deep snow. He showed me how to track the rabbits and find them huddled in the snow banks. I felt a bit sorry for the poor rabbits, but they really tasted good. We had fun killing rats that frequented the garbage bin on the back side of the property. They were huge wharf rats. We would go down to the barrel and rock it a bit and the rats would scurry out. At first I was to stand with a club and hit them as they ran out, but I missed every time, so John told me to rock the barrel and he would hit them. He killed nine rats one afternoon. I told him it was too bad that those nasty things were not good to eat. (I have since learned that in parts of the world, people do eat rats, but I still do not find them appealing.)

As time passed, I began to miss going to school. The sparkling newness of the marriage adventure began to wear off, and I wondered where my life was really headed. It was so nice to have someone to love and care about me, but I wanted better things for us both than life in a junk yard. John worked hard, but timber work is seasonal and offered little for the future. I loved to learn and yearned to gain skills. I remembered how my sister-in-law could crochet such beautiful pineapple doilies and tablecloths, rose bedspreads, multicolored vests that reminded me of Joseph's coat, purses, and other things. I would learn that. I went uptown and bought a beginners book, some thread, and a crochet needle. It didn't take long to learn the basic single, double, and triple stitches. I turned out a small change purse and a couple of doilies. I didn't have the rhythm or nimbleness of a professional, and my products looked amateurish, but I improved with each new effort. I also bought a tatting shuttle and taught myself the ancient art of tatting. Some days I would just walk to uptown Benton and window shop for an hour or two.

Chapter 11

Cotton-picking Venture

That winter, John was laid off from Farm Bureau sawmill. The mill was going out of business so it didn't need logs. Some of John's friends decided to go to Oregon where there was lots of timber work. John and I talked about going out there, but didn't want to just set out with no prospects for a job or place to stay. At least here, we had friends.

In the summer of 1951, John and I, along with a neighbor, Mr. Frankenberry, decided we would go up to north Arkansas, pick a load of peaches, and peddle them around to make some extra money. People had little money to buy. We eventually had a lot of overripe peaches that we had to throw away or give to people who could use them right away. We decided that selling fresh produce was not our forte.

Our next venture involved a trip to Kennett, Missouri. John had two sisters that lived there, and they informed us that cotton picking was in season and we could make money there.

We moved in with June and her husband and looked about for work. Cotton was good that year, and John could pick well over 200lb. a day. I did well to get 100 lb. At $3.00 per hundred pounds that would give us about $10 a day total for both of us. It was backbreaking work, but we were happy to get it. After frost fell, we pulled bolls. It was amazing to watch John pulling bolls. He kept a steady stream of bolls moving from the stalks to his cotton sack He could pull in excess of 1000 lb. a day. He and his sister, Lucille, competed to see who could pull the most. They both were very good, but I did well to get 200 lb. Boll pulling did not pay as much per pound, but was still not too bad. Soon John got a job driving a combine to harvest wheat and soybeans. I was still working the field. Winter came on, and work opportunities died down. I think the best thing about the Missouri stay was getting to spend time with June and her family and with the Kellogg family. John's sister, Lucille and her husband, Rick had five boisterous children. They all worked hard picking cotton during the week, and Lucille and Rick would reward them with a Saturday night drive-in movie along with lots of soda pop and snacks. The drive-in proprietors charged per person for multiple persons in an automobile. The two younger kids, Becky and Jerry, would lie down in the back seat, and the two older ones Bob and Betty, would sit on top of them until they got past the ticket office. As soon as the car parked, they all hopped out with their snacks and positioned themselves on the ground to enjoy the show.

On one occasion, John and I went with them and helped pay ticket fees for everyone. We saw *The Three Stooges*, and *Dumbo the Flying Elephant*. What a treat and wonderful diversion from the cotton patch. The elephant story was so cute and one of

Walt Disney's first animated films. A mother elephant (I think her name was Mrs. Jumbo) promised a bird (Maisie) that she would sit on her bird egg until Maisie could take a short rest and find some food. Once relieved from duty, the bird flew away and left the poor elephant sitting on the egg for months on end. Through snow and rain she sat there determined to keep her promise to keep the egg warm until the bird returned.

What a lesson in being faithful to one's promise! Finally, the egg hatched! Mrs. Jumbo was most pleasantly surprised and rewarded for her faithful effort. Various Disney productions, that have delighted audiences of all ages, have since been made from this story.

Another special day with the Kelloggs was the Fourth of July 1951. We all went fishing on a nearby river. Rick loved to jug fish. He had a large number of plastic milk jugs on which he had a short line and hook. After getting in his boat, he baited the hooks and released the jugs all at one time on the river. He joyfully paddled after the jugs as they floated downstream. If one stopped floating and started bobbing, he knew he had a fish. Rick had a wooden peg leg that was a major part of his personality. He would dangle the peg over the edge of the boat and chant. With his ruddy complexion, he was the very essence of a friendly pirate.

CHAPTER 12

Back to Sheridan and Family Fun

As summer work wound down, John and I decided we were homesick for the people back home. I had never been away from my family for so long, so we saved money enough to make the return trip. Back in Arkansas, John went to work hauling paper wood again. Mrs. Reeder, a neighbor to Mildred and J. Harrington, had recently been widowed and wanted to move to Little Rock to be near her daughter. She offered to let John and I live in her house rent free until she decided what she wanted to do with it.

I loved it there. The Harrington's seven kids were a joy to me. I was 17 and not much more than a child myself. Sandy, their little girl was about three or four by this time. She had fine puffy blond hair that was as soft as duck's down. When she slept on it at night, it kind of wadded behind her head, and she would pat it proudly thinking it was a curl. She would often stuff her little rag doll under her arm and sneak up the road to my house. Her mother would panic when she found her missing, but soon figured out where she was. We were all afraid she would get run over in the road, so everyone watched out for her. Sometimes her brother, Michael (Mike) would come with her. He was about a couple of years older than Sandy, but seemed as wise and serious as an old man. They played under the big shade tree in front of my house. I would sit in the window watching them and eavesdrop on their conversations. Sandy had a crush on a neighbor teen-age boy who was so "fine" with dark wavy hair and a winning smile. She confided to Mike one day that she was going to marry that boy. Mike said sourly in his sternest 5-year-old voice, "Aw, Sandy, you can't get married 'til you start to school."

The Harrington boys all loved their Uncle John and would come running to our house the minute he came home from work. I always had supper ready, and John insisted that they all eat with us. I was not accustomed to cooking for or expecting so many "guests", so I just kept opening up cans of stuff, adding a little water, and serving it up. They could gobble up a week's worth of groceries in a few minutes. We all enjoyed each other, though, and it really didn't matter. Mildred often sent eggs, milk, and canned goods to help us.

John and J. would regularly take the boys coon or squirrel hunting. That was the talk of every get-together. The boys had an old shotgun that kicked like a wild mule. When the dogs treed something, they all lined up behind the leading boy, who was usually Jim or Roy, and held on tight while the shotgun was blasted off. Then they all fell backwards like a stack of dominoes.

During holidays, I would help Mildred in the kitchen. She always had lots of good recipes. Jenny Katherine, the oldest girl, helped with everything her mother did. Mildred had a firm work ethic and taught that well to all her children. The family always grew a large garden and canned a thousand jars of produce during the growing season. They raised lots of Irish potatoes which they aired out in the shade of a big oak tree and used for almost every meal.

Christmas that year was even skimpier than the one before. John had the mumps. It made him mad at first when we said he had the mumps because he thought only kids had mumps. It didn't take long for him to admit his condition, though, because both sides of his face swelled to a strut. He sent money by Mildred to get a Christmas present for me, but she didn't find the things he requested, sp she brought the money back. I got nothing for Christmas that year. John felt really bad about that. I tried to make him feel better by telling him that he gave me enough last year for two years anyway.

Mildred and J. had two more children for a total of nine. Pat was the youngest girl. She was a cute little tomboy. So much so that she asked her dad to give her a GI haircut like the boys had. To Mildred's chagrin, he did it. Pat wore a turban on her head until it grew back to a decent length.

When the youngest boy was born, there was such a commotion among the kids about what to name him that he wound up being Tommy Joe David Harrington. Oddly enough, he has always been known as Butch. Once, Mildred asked me to keep him while she and J. went to town to take care of some business. They were gone much longer than expected and Butch began to get hungry and started crying. Since Mildred breast fed him, I prayed she would return soon, but the clock kept ticking and Butch kept crying. I looked around for something to feed him. Mildred said there was some banana pudding in a cabinet that she had hid from Jimmy, but I could not find it. Finally I spied a jar of her homemade pickles. I got one to eat myself and Butch kept looking at it. Finally I let him suck some of the pickle juice from it and he drifted off to sleep. When she came home she was surprised to find the baby sleeping peacefully.

We lived in Mrs. Reeder's house only a few months until she sold it to Noel Gentry and we had to move again. This time we moved near Palestine on a place owned by Cole Walters and his Aunt, Arbell Burton. The house was old and made with wide pine clapboards that had aged and weathered through the years. It had a front porch that extended the length of the house in front and had a boarded dug well on the left end of the porch. A "dog trot" opening separated the two main sections of the house. The property had been owned by Mr. Melvin Walters who had died in a drowning accident a few years before. Some of his belongings were still in the house, so the owners stored everything on the right side and rented us the two rooms on the left side of the house.

The rustic old house was nestled among trees in an idyllic setting, but was so remote that I was somewhat frightened out there by myself all day while John was at work. I could hear all kinds of noises coming from the squeaky house. I needed a clothes line as our clothes were still hand washed and approached John about arranging to put one up for me. There was a low hanging telephone line connected to the house which we thought had no current since we did not have a phone. John suggested I hang my clothes on that until he could get some wire and posts. I got out there one morning and did the wash. When I flopped a big bed sheet over the telephone wire, it almost jarred all my teeth loose. For a moment, I could not let go. With a few adjustments, I soon got used to living in the "wild" and busied myself with making a garden, canning, and taking care of the yard. My dad brought his plow horse over and plowed my garden for me. He still lived at Belfast and knew a shortcut through the woods to my house about two miles away.

At times, I still missed school and attempted to learn more skills on my own again. I found an old high school typing book and decided to learn to type. Since I didn't have a typewriter, I drew out a keyboard on a thick piece of flat cardboard and used that to practice. I followed all the exercises in the book and was amazed at how my fingers could find the locations of the letters. I typed with both hands in this game I created with a make-believe typewriter. I knew exactly when I made a mistake and would practice the patterns over and over until I could do them correctly. I am sure it gave me a similar pleasure that many find in doing different kinds of puzzles.

John liked to hunt, and we had a good squirrel/coon dog we dubbed "Ole Spike." Spike became the child we didn't yet have. We showered him with attention and love, and he reciprocated as only a dog can. He came in and out of the house at will and slept by the wood heater in the living room. He helped to keep wild meat of all kinds on our table when we could not afford to buy meat from the butcher section of the grocery stores. Spike made me feel so much safer when I was alone.

Besides Spike, John gradually accumulated a pen full of dogs of various mixed breeds and sizes. At that time it was customary to drive a pack of dogs through the woods to cause a deer to jump up and run. Howling and barking, the dogs gave chase. Hunters would station themselves at various points to get a good shot as the deer ran out. During deer season, many of John's friends would bring tents and set up in the woods near our house to take part in the action. They liked a large number of dogs for the chase, so they began bringing dogs down and leaving them. They usually brought a sack of feed and promised to bring more as needed, but very few sacks of feed were brought after the initial one. We were stuck with feeding all the dogs.

One day when the dog feed was low and there was very little food in our own house, John took the dogs down into the woods to see if he could kill a deer. They struck up a trail and soon a young deer jumped out. John shot it! The dogs ravenously tore into it. John tried to control them and finally tied their collars together with a piece of rope and led them growling and resisting back to the house and put them in their pen. He proceeded to return to the woods to get the deer, but when he got back to the spot, the dogs had dug under the fence and beat him back down there. They had eaten almost the entire animal by that time. John was so disgusted because he had hoped to get at least a tender steak or two from the carcass.

It was during this time that I noticed smoke billowing up east over Belfast way. Uncle Joe's store and home had caught fire and burnt to ashes. Some time before that Wilbanks' place had burned. Belfast was not the same. Activity gradually slowed down, and people began to move away to find better opportunities. Ethel Covington now had the post office near her home across the track. Soon the post office was taken out.

CHAPTER 13

Sawmilling- A Family Venture

Before *we married, John had operated a* sawmill on Tucker Mountain near Birdtown. His brother-in-law, Bossie Cullins had helped him, and they made pretty good money on the lumber they cut. John got the idea that he would get another mill and do as well with it in Grant County where there was bigger, taller timber. We had little money for the venture, but he went up near Morrilton and found an old "ground hog mill". The timbers had decayed on it until there was little left but a pile of scrap iron. John was overjoyed when he dumped the rusty iron pieces into our front yard. I didn't want to be a killjoy so didn't say very much, but thought he was in for a big disappointment to try to make anything out of that heap. He set to work building new timbers to support the rails, sharpened the saw blade, and soon had it set up. Everyone admired it, including myself. John could do anything.

We still had no power source. John found an old diesel engine that was about as dilapidated as the mill had been. He tore it apart and overhauled the engine. It purred like a kitten. He leased a tract of timber and set up the mill. He managed to get two work horses and a log wagon, hired some half dozen people to help him, and began to saw logs. I went to watch the maiden voyage, but soon was hooked into doodling slabs down a ramp to a burning pile and off-bearing lumber and cross ties. I loved the scent of fresh sawn lumber and enjoyed being a part of the venture. We had willing helpers, people who were desperate for work and happy to be with us. Even though John was gifted with a talent for mechanical things, he knew very little about marketing the products and figuring the costs of labor, horse feed, and upkeep of the mill. We worked hard, but saw little profit.

At one time, John's brother-in-law, J. Harrington came to help out with his personal work force of four boys, Jimmy, Roy, Larry, and Billy Wayne. The boys knew how to work and followed instructions well. It was so difficult and expensive to keep all the equipment in working order that the mill was never profitable. It did, however, teach us some very good lessons in economy as we struggled along for almost four years.

One fall, John's sister Louise and her family were down on their luck, so John hired Earl to work with him at the mill. Earl stayed with us a few days while his family remained in Birdtown. Earl was looking for a place to live when our landlords graciously consented to clear the two rooms on the east side of the house for these new tenants. They boxed up the dog-trot hallway and stored the deceased owner's things in there. Soon Earl, Louise and their four children: Martha

Ann, Mary Ruth, Benny Earl, and Sarah Jane were settled in next door. They were a wonderful, fun family, and I was glad to have them close by. Mary Ruth and Benny Earl were enrolled in Sheridan Schools. Martha Ann and I took care of most of the chores around the house, and Louise cared for Sarah Jane, who was still a toddler and just beginning to talk. And talk she did! To our embarrassment she picked up on every loose word said in her presence. That taught us to be more careful about what we said. Another thing Sarah Jane liked was magazines, especially the *National Geographic* with lots of pictures. She found a picture of a scantily clad indigenous native woman nursing a child in one of them. She showed that picture to everybody that came around saying it was Aunt Lossie. She would giggle and her eyes would sparkle with mischievousness. Needless to say, I hid that magazine at the first opportunity.

There was never a dull moment! Martha Ann liked to dress up in old clothes to look like a tramp and slip through the woods to the main road and come slouching up the path to our house trying to make us think a stranger was calling. She would spook the horses and dogs causing them to run about wildly and set up a deafening noise. One of the dogs was fooled enough that he darted out intending to go through a hole in the fence, but missed the hole and fell over backwards stunned from the impact.

Martha Ann had a great sense of humor and a lively imagination! The effects of her humor were also sometimes frustrating to me. She loved to slip around to the back of the outhouse when it was occupied and run a stick in an opening at the back to lightly poke whoever was using the privy at the time. Since snakes frequented places like that, the first thing an occupant would think was "snake!" With the important business so untimely interrupted, occupant burst out of the door hurriedly adjusting clothes only to be met with Martha Ann's familiar giggling hee-hee-hee. I was usually the butt of this joke, and began to try to use the toilet as little as possible. That not being a good solution health wise, I decided I would find some secret places in the woods to frequent.

Martha Ann was relentless in her quest for fun. I was a few years older than she and tried to be as tolerant as possible. After all, I was the "older" (18) married woman who should have more understanding. I prided myself in taking all in good spirits. I was perfectly capable of retaliation, but wanted it at the right time in the right way. Soon, I had my chance. Earl and John had gone coon hunting one night. They arrived home about 5 a.m. with two coons in tow sacks. It was almost time for them to go to work, so John stashed the dead coons under our bed and went to work. Later that morning Martha Ann came over. She and I were talking about the coons that were under the bed. Since coon hides would bring 50 cents each, we decided we would skin them and tack the hides on the smoke house to dry. We had both watched the guys do this so much that we thought we could do it. We spread newspapers on the floor near the heater and dragged the sacks containing the coons out. We opened the sacks and emptied the coons on the newspaper. I had sharpened the butcher knife, and while she held the first coon by the hind legs, I scored the belly. Greasy blobs of fat oozed out from the sliced opening. We carefully stripped off the hide and lay the naked coon on the newspaper. Martha Ann sat it up and crossed its hands on its swollen belly.

We both laughed because it looked like a newborn baby just emerged from the womb. Then she got an idea. She grabbed the coon and ran down the porch. She sat it up in front of the door and knocked. She then ran around to the side of the house and waited. Her mother opened the door. When she saw the posing coon, she was at first horrified; then she realized what it was. Martha Ann popped out from around the house and laughed.

That done, Martha Ann returned to the business at hand. We still had another coon to skin. We set back to work, laughing and joking all the time. We had almost completed the second skinning when Martha Ann suddenly had another idea. She picked up the first carcass again and warped me over the head. Fat dripped off my long hair and into my face. I couldn't believe she had done that, but she was laughing so hard and pointing. I thought to myself, "Well, now is the time to see if she can take what she puts out." I quickly made the final two slices on the second coon, snatched up the carcass and returned her attack. I thought how ridiculous we both must look dripping with coon fat and blood as we continued the charade. Martha Ann was true to character. She could take whatever she put out. I was trying to take the "conflict" outside to save my living room from further damage; so still waving the burdensome, ungodly weapon, I dashed for the door and ran down the porch. An idea struck me. I would whisk into their room and hide. I ran in and got behind the door. Louise, hearing the commotion, stuck her head out to see what was going on. Martha Ann, mistakenly thinking it was me coming back, smacked her right in the face with the coon carcass. She yelled, "Martha Ann, I'm going to tell Earl on you." Soon Louise, too, was laughing uncontrollably, wiping off coon grease, and remarking what a nice skin softener it was. We spent the entire day cleaning up our mess. The well had gone dry, and we had to carry water from a spring a mile away. After that, I relaxed more with Martha Ann and loved her more than ever. I knew she was not going to be mad at me if I got her back for her antics. She knew I could be ornery, too, so it kept her humor somewhat in check. That was our first and only coon fight, but it made an unbelievable memory to relive at family gatherings for years to come. I learned that no matter how poor the circumstances people can enjoy each other and have lots of fun.

Bennie Earl was doing well in school. He had made friends in his class with Sid McMath's son, Philip. Bennie liked to play and roughhouse with the dogs. He found an old tire and liked to jump on it and ride it over. One Sunday, as the family was all sitting in the yard, he was showing us his skill. "Look at me," he said as he made a perfect turn over the top of the tire. We all turned to look as he fell on the second turn. He grabbed his arm and complained briefly. Earl and John thought he was ok because he could still move his fingers. His arm swelled during the night, and his temperature was elevated. He stayed home from school the next day, and Louise gave him aspirin for the pain. He was restless all day and came in and out to see me. I made him some cookies.

That evening Earl and John took him to Dr. Carter's office. The Doctor x-rayed the arm and found it was broken in two places. They had to set it. The pain was so severe that Bennie upchucked all the food we had pampered him with all day. He was proud of his cast, though, and had all his classmates autograph it when he went back to school. Mary Ruth started to school, but felt ill at ease. She was a quiet, loving child who seemed to be staunchly independent.

The Hendersons stayed for about eight or ten months, then moved back to Birdtown where Earl went to work for the DeLaney Cattle Farm. I really missed them because it left me alone way out in the woods by myself during the day when John was working. I am a gregarious person and function better around people. John continued the sawmill work with various people laboring with him to eke out a subsistence.

CHAPTER 14

Spiritual and Economical Change

John and I always dreamed of owning our own place. We hoped to buy some land and eventually build a house. At length, we bought about three-quarters of an acre from Emmett Smith on State Highway 35 about a mile north of Palestine Church. Mr. Smith had once owned a foundry up north, but he and his wife had retired to Arkansas. He was a kindly old gentleman who loved his big shaggy dog. His wife was stricken with some kind of illness that caused her to require a hot fire in her room every day even in hot summertime. The old fellow would build her a fire in the wood heater then retire to the shade tree in the yard to try to catch a breeze now and then. He was glad to have us as neighbors and let us pay the land out at $25.00 a month until we paid a total of $125. James Kentner, one of John's friends sold us an old 16x16 ft. center-pole army tent to live in. We dug a well and set up. We had hopes of saving and building a modest little house on the property, but we could not accumulate enough money to do very much toward that dream. The tent was cozy. We had a wood heater, a refrigerator, a kerosene cook stove, studio couch, bed, table, and a couple of mismatched chairs. All the items were our pride and joy because we had to scrimp and save for each one. We had bought the refrigerator on credit with a down payment of the silver dollars John had given me the week after we were married. I sold a pig I had raised to make the first payment. On most days we could raise the tent flaps to get light and air, but we had one electric light bulb and a small electric fan. It was almost luxurious for an adventurous young couple like we were.

One night John and I walked to a neighbor's house to watch wrestling on their black and white television. Coming home late, we entered the tent to see a black chicken snake with its head over a bucket of eggs I had left sitting near the refrigerator. The snake was frightened and tried to jerk back under the refrigerator, but he had already swallowed three eggs and the bumps they made scotched his retreat as he yanked his body desperately to break the eggs inside him. John killed the snake. It measured four feet long.

We lived in the tent for three years. During this time, John and I both began attending church at Belfast again. I was glad to be back in my old church. I had never been baptized because I was not clear on what God really required of me and did not think I could live his holy standards. One day Reverend Joe Poe came by and talked to us about the atonement Jesus had made for us. I finally understood that I had to personalize the sacrifice, believe that Christ died for me, repent, and accept the gift he so freely offered. I felt like a new person. The bitterness that had often entered my heart, seemed to melt away and in its place was love and compassion for others. What a marvelous, simple plan I had overlooked. I wanted to follow my Lord in baptism and try to live so that my life would show the love I felt for him. John and I were both baptized the same day in the Selton Jordan pond near Belfast. Life was good and had a purpose.

I thought I could feel the spirit leading us in the days and weeks to come. John finally got a much better job working for Reynolds and Williams road Construction Company. The gravel road (State Highway 35) by our tent was going to be paved. John first worked picking up roots behind the equipment then was elevated to driving a sprinkler truck days and helping the "grease monkey" nights. His boss, Mr. Homer Carder, soon found out that John was a talented mechanic so he gave him a job as a mechanic's helper. After a time, the mechanic had a heart attack and had to retire. John was made head mechanic. It was amazing how he managed to do that without being able to read and write. He was making $2.00 an hour and with lots of overtime, we saved over $1000 that first summer.

Meantime, I kept wondering if there was not a better way for me. I had taught myself to type and considered taking a secretarial course, but had no way to get to school. We had no car, and I could not drive anyway. Finally I signed up with American School of Chicago for a correspondence course to finish two years of high school. Every day I took my books outside the tent and spread them on a little table under an oak tree. I tackled math, science, history and literature. For literature the required novel was *Giants in the Earth* by Rolvaag. That novel somehow inspired me because it told about the endurance of people who settled on the western prairie. Some lived in mud huts. Life was so hard and the people so poor and isolated that the mother of the family had a difficult time holding on to her sanity. I began to realize that the struggle for survival is universal. There is no luxury of giving up. By working hard at that course, I finished in about four months. What a door that opened for me! With John's loving support, we got an apartment near Little Rock Junior College (now UALR), and I had the privilege of actually going to college. My efforts were not always understood by the gentle God-fearing people in my community. I knew that education for me was the only way out of abject poverty, and. I wanted to go to school so badly that I would have willingly slept on the sidewalk if necessary.

When I took my American School diploma up to the college and asked for admission, they informed me I would have to take a battery of tests to see if I qualified for placement. The test was a timed test about four hours long. My heart raced and my hands were clammy as I tried to beat the deadlines and answer all the questions that I could. When the proctor said "Stop," I was so lost in concentration that I jumped almost out of my chair. They gathered the scantrons and said they would let us know in about a week. I had to know today if possible because we had to look for an apartment near the school if I passed; if not, I would go dejected back to the tent and try to recover my dignity. Desperately, I went to the dean's office and explained my situation. He kindly said he would go check it out and see if he could get my results immediately. I sat praying and waiting for what seemed an eternity, but was probably only about ten minutes. The Dean reappeared smiling and told me I had done quite well on the test, and that he would see me in school in the weeks to come. Joy swelled in my whole body! I felt like dancing! I would get a chance to prove myself!

The next day we searched for an apartment near the school. Our friends Verdieree and Minor Cullins went with us, and we made it a day. We drove around and looked within twenty blocks of Little Rock Junior College on all sides. About one o'clock we drove past a fruit stand on Asher Avenue. We were all hungry, and I remarked that the big stalks of bananas looked so lucious. We had no money, but John joked that he would drive back by there in a few minutes and let me look again. We all laughed, knowing that all that any of us could do was salivate.

Finally, we found a single room at Rock-a-way Court near the college so I could walk to school as I still did not know how to drive. It had just a bed and a tiny bath with shower and commode. An electric hot plate enabled me to fix snacks and boil coffee. I started classes in January of 1957. It didn't take me long to realize that college would not be as easy as high school was for me. These students were serious about getting an education, and competition was keen. In my speech class, there were about twenty veterans returning from the Korean War and attending school on the GI Bill. I admired them as world travelers and often felt intimidated by their abilities to articulate. I sometimes doubted my own ability to measure up.

So many interesting things happened. In my music appreciation class, I met a blind student who had been a welder. Joe had lost his sight to diabetes. He could get around campus with his cane by following the sidewalks. He was in my biology class and was assigned to be my lab partner. He was such a positive, likeable person that I usually forgot about his being blind. Joe and his wife moved into a trailer behind the apartments where I lived. They came over one night to visit John and me. They brought a delicious apple pie she had baked herself. It was sugar-free with a thin slice of cheese on it. She cooked special desserts like this one because of Joe's diabetes. After we enjoyed the pie and talked a while, they asked if I would mind if Joe walked to school with me.

I was glad to have him walk along, but had the idea I would lead him. When we walked, he touched my elbow lightly with his left hand and used his cane with his right hand. It was like any two friends walking and chatting together. Joe helped me tremendously in the music appreciation class. We studied classical music which I had never known anything about. Joe listened to classical musical all the time at home. He hummed the themes to me on the way to school. He would say, "This is *Beethoven's Fifth Symphony*" and boom out the wakening sound. He knew the Sultan and Scheherazade themes, *Till Oilenspiel* with the clatter of chickens in the marketplace, and could imitate the marching of Roman soldiers in *The Pines of Rome*. He had a wealth of wonderful things in his mind. In biology class, I described the paramecium and amoeba that I saw in the microscope while he punched out his notes in Braille. We made a great scholar team. Joe hoped to become a counselor, and soon the powers that be decided to waiver the biology lab requirement because of his being blind. It really was not a course he needed for his profession anyway.

Another of the amazing things about Joe was how he helped with the laundry. His wife would sort the clothes into different bags according to color and he would take them to the laundry room and wash them on a wringer-type washing machine. He could fill the rinse tub and swing the wringer around wherever he needed it. He rarely asked for help and never had an accident. He managed his paper money by folding the bills different ways according to their denominations and knew coins by feel. I felt truly blessed to know him.

I continued the biology class and was assigned another lab partner. Once, we anesthetized a small frog, took its heart out and put it in a salt solution where it continued to beat for hours. We dissected a huge embalmed frog (We dubbed her Betsy because she was full of eggs.) and learned all the inside parts. I loved doing that. I had killed chickens and prepared dishes with them at home, so the frog thing didn't seem a lot different. My partner assigned to that project was a young girl from Bryant, Arkansas. She didn't want to touch the frog, and was revolted by the smell of the embalming fluid. That was ok with me. I search through the innards and found blue veins and red arteries which had been filled with dye for easy identification. I was so fascinated that I would eagerly relate to John every evening what we did in biology class that day. He listened with rapt attention. So much so that it caused him to have a horrible dream. He woke up one night and was so angry with me. I had never seen him so angry in the seven years we had been married. I asked him what was wrong as he emerged from his hypnotic-like state. He softened toward me and explained that he dreamed that I had dissected his dog to see what was inside.

I wasn't really that bad, but I did have some mischievous moments. One day we were examining a life-sized human skeleton that was dangling by the head from a rack. We were supposed to learn all the bone structure of the body. My lab friend, being careful not to touch the skeleton, was making notes at a distance of about a foot and a half. She bent down to examine the toes when I got this idea. I raised the skeleton's arm and placed it ever so gently on her head. She screamed so loud that I could have sworn the skeleton turned red with embarrassment. She ran from the room with several students chasing her to see what the matter was. Soon she came back in, both arms supported on each side by two students. Drained white by the fright, she sat down weakly. I was truly sorry I had scared her so badly. She was a good sport, and in a few days, could laugh about the whole matter.

CHAPTER 15

An After-school Job, School Honors, and Interrupted Plans

In the late spring, I decided to try to get an after-school job because John had been laid off during the winter, and we were pinching pennies to meet our bills. Mr. Gatlin, Manager of the Sterling Store at Town and Country Shopping Center, gave me my first real job. The store was just over the hill from the college and I could walk to work. I was working there during the Central High Crisis. Some of the clerks who worked with me were girls who were still going to High School at Central. It was a very tense time for them. Government troops came in to protect the students during the integration of the school. Nine black students braved the crisis and finished the semester.

During the fall semester, I made all A's and was invited to join the Phi Theta Kappa Honor Society. I was honored to be invited, but was going to decline because the initiation required a fee and a formal dress for a banquet in our honor. I had no idea how I could arrange for the things I needed. I confided to one of my friends, Mary Levy, about the invitation, and she was thrilled. She said I must not decline. That afternoon she and her mother came by with a lovely gold-colored formal, gold slippers, and a golden beaded clutch purse. To top off the outfit, they had included matching jewelry. I was awestruck. Never had I been dressed so fine.

The banquet was to be at the Hotel Marion in downtown Little Rock (It has since been imploded). John was going to drive me in his old work truck which was covered with grease and dust. We cleaned it as best we could and laid a quilt over the seat to protect my finery. We set out to go downtown, but John was so confused by the one-way streets that after driving around and around, he finally stopped at Wright's Service Station on Broadway and called a taxi for me. He waited there until I returned. I felt like Cinderella when I alighted from the cab. The guys from the chapter were dressed in tuxedos. They escorted the ladies to the ballroom. They pulled out my chair for me and I sat down to a table set with formal china and an array of silverware that stretched out from the plate in both directions. I was truly dazzled by the lovely furnishings and hardly knew what to do. Then I remembered some advice that my home economics teacher had given me in high school. She had told us to follow the host or hostess when we were unsure of ourselves. I watched our sponsor's every move, and was soon enjoying myself. Soon it was time to go. I hurried out to the lobby and asked someone to call a cab (I didn't know how to use a phone) to take me back to where John was waiting. We both laughed as though it were all a comedy of errors.

CHAPTER 16

A Miracle Child

In the spring of 1958, I began to feel tired all the time. I was nauseated in the mornings, had little energy, and wanted to do nothing but sleep. My whole body seemed to be going through a transformation. I went to the doctor who determined that I was pregnant. It was hard to believe that had happened after seven years of marriage. I was happy to finally become a mother, but didn't know how I could afford to continue my college work and pay the expenses of having a baby.

I finished the spring semester and summer terms completing my sophomore year and went to join my husband who was working an asphalt job in Junction City, Arkansas. We moved into the upstairs part of an old hotel. The Romeros, a Spanish family, lived across the hall. We each had three rooms divided by a long hall with one bathroom at the upper end. I loved the Romeros. There was Modesto and his wife, Pat, Alice, and Jeanie. Mrs. Romero, giving me much needed and appreciated advice on how to care for myself before the baby came, was like a mother to me. She had recently lost her daughter Rosa in a tragic event and seemed to compensate for her loss by trying to help me. She had given birth to several children and assured me there was "nothing" to be afraid of." My new doctor, Wilbur West, said it was a very natural thing and encouraged me to read books on natural child birth. His favorite expression seemed to be "When the apple is ripe, it will fall." With that encouragement, I was not worried.

While I waited for the baby to come, I enrolled in correspondence work from the University of Arkansas. I had completed two years of French language in the classroom so thought that taking a correspondence class in French would help me keep up my skills. A Grigsby family, who had three lovely girls ranging in age from five to fourteen, lived downstairs. The two smallest girls, Nita and Dalton, spent lots of time with me. Nita, who was about eight, wanted me to teach her some French words. I was glad to have someone to practice on, and we began to try our vocabulary on each other, delighting in the expressions. I finished two courses in French and one in American Government.

By December, my body had enlarged from 140 to 162 lb. I was a huge blimp. The baby inside me seemed to take great pleasure in kicking and squirming during the wee hours of the night. December passed and no birth occurred; January, and still no child. I thought of how Hannah had pleaded with God for a child before Samuel was born. He had answered her prayers, and she dedicated her child to Him. I decided that, I too, would dedicate my child to God albeit not in the same way that Hannah had done. I promised Him that I would teach my child to know and love Heavenly Father. He had answered my prayer, but here my faith seemed to waver. Why did it take so long? The doctor had diagnosed my pregnancy in June saying he already was hearing a heart beat and that I was probably about four months along. Would the baby be healthy when it finally arrived? In weak moments, I even wondered if I really had a baby inside me, or was this some kind of unusual growth or trick that fate was playing on me. I was soon to find out for sure.

On February 1, 1959, I got up after a restless night. My body was aching all over. I went to the doctor, and he thought I was beginning to dilate. He said it was time to go to the Warner Brown Hospital in El Dorado, Arkansas. Dr. West sat at the desk and waited as I was put in a room and told to walk and walk and walk. The clock kept ticking and ticking and ticking. The pain was severe, and I kept thinking "relax, relax, relax" as I was told to do. Finally, about 10 p.m. he decided to hasten events by breaking my water. There was no water. It had broken almost two weeks before and I had not known that was what was happening.

My birth canal was too small for such a big baby. The doctor called in a specialist. He made incisions and used forceps to extract the baby. Finally you appeared at about 1 a.m. on February, 2, 1959. (My little ground hog) You weighed in at 10 lb. 12 ½ ounces and measured 24 inches long. John was so happy that he cried. He had been fearful of losing me and the baby. I had been so weary that I had almost given up until a loud, rude voice from a distraught doctor had said, "Push, dammit, push." I think that jarred me enough that I began trying to help. You were bruised and your little head was indented on both sides by the forceps. I prayed you would be ok, but you were mine, and I loved you so much. In about a couple of weeks, you blossomed out into a plump, well-formed baby. You were my miracle. I was so grateful.

After that, the thought of having another child was not a good idea to me. The "apple" did not always fall when it was ripe. I would just enjoy the blessing I had and not worry about a larger family. I really idolized you and thought you would surely be the smartest kid on any block. The road crew that John worked with doted on you also. You got to play after hours on the "big machines" while pretending to be a dragline or dozer operator. As you grew bigger, John would sometimes take you out on the job and let you play in the huge piles of dirt. You loved to get really greasy and dirty because it made you think you were working like the big guys.

Wherever we moved, I would take you to church as often as I could. I wanted you to know God and to be able to make good choices as you grew up. As most parents, I wanted you to have things and opportunities like I had not had. I stayed home and cared for you until you were a year old. Then I started back to school.

In the summer of 1960, we lived at Blytheville. I decided to take classes at Jonesboro, Arkansas. I got an apartment just off campus, and my dad came up and stayed with me to baby sit while I was in class. Dad's hobby for years had been whittling out six-piece puzzle balls in his spare time. He made a big one about the size of a softball for you. He bought a red ball cap for his little "Slugger," and you two sallied forth every morning with Dad pushing the stroller around campus and you enjoying the ride. The puzzle ball, which you always carried in your dimpled hands, was the object of many impromptu conversations with the people you met on campus. Everyone soon knew the old man and the little boy in the red cap. We often joked about your starting at the college level before you entered first grade. John was working at Blytheville and we went home to see him on Wednesdays and week-ends.

The superintendent of school at the Blytheville Air Force Base contacted me at semester's end and asked me to teach at the base during the fall semester. He said I was eligible to get a 90-hour permit. I tentatively agreed to teach fourth grade but was hesitant because I had wanted to be a high school teacher. Also, he gave me neither textbooks in order to plan my classes nor a contract to sign. Evidently, I was just supposed to show up on the first day of school and face the students. About two weeks before school started, John was transferred to Stuttgart. I had to resign the offer to teach, or I would spend the winter alone at Blytheville.

As it happened, we no more than got settled in Stuttgart than John was transferred back to Blytheville for the winter. I was alone anyway. The road crew that remained in Stuttgart was very supportive. Roy and Audrey Harrington lived just a few blocks away, and their son Dewaine was about your age. Retha and Pat Romero lived rather close, too, so they were a great help to me. I was somewhat fearful at living alone and wondered what I would do in a case of emergency. One day, I was cleaning house and heard a knock at my back door. I noticed a pick-up truck out front and wondered why someone would go to the back. The knock came again very insistently. I opened the door and a huge black man stepped up in the threshold. I was so frightened that I ran screaming through the house, quickly grabbed you up in my arms, and was headed out the front door. The man was just as frightened as I was. He said, "No, Ma'am; no Ma'am! Nothing like that!" I stopped briefly and listened to his explanation. He had come there to see a policeman who had formerly lived in that house. He said the policeman had severely reprimanded him with lots of expletives for coming to his front door and admonished him to always come to the back door when visiting a white person. I told him he needed to come to my front door. I was sorry I had been so scared and apologized for shaking him up as well. After he made profuse apologies, he left and then stopped by a neighbor's house a few minutes later. She knew the man and joked that he had turned white and was still shaking.

Spring soon came and John was transferred to Jacksonville where we gladly joined him. We lived in a house on Valentine Road. Roy and Audrey moved in with us for a short time as Roy was still working on the road crew. I decided to take classes at Arkansas State Teachers College (now UCA) that summer. Colleges required that students spend their last year of school on one campus to get a degree. UCA was centrally located; it seemed a good choice. I enrolled for classes that summer. I rented an apartment near the campus, and Dad again came to help me with Claud. What a blessing Dad was! Audrey was a good cook and she and Roy helped John survive while I was away. Once when they were gone for a few days, John went out to get some groceries that he could fix for himself. He could not read the labels, but knew he liked Campbell's soup. He bought a case of what he thought was vegetable soup but turned out to be mushroom soup. I asked him why he threw some of it in the commode and he said, "Because it looked like that's where it belonged." He had thought it was spoiled. He could always enjoy a good laugh on himself. Luckily, he never lost his wonderful sense of humor in all the health struggles he had in years to follow.

CHAPTER 17

First Teaching Jobs

At UCA that summer, I met Fayburn Smith, Superintendent of Enola School District, who was in my history class. (Enola is about 20 miles northeast of Conway.) He needed a high school teacher to teach English and history from 7th to 12th grades. I finally had a teaching job! This time I intended to see it through. I would begin with a 90-hour teaching certificate. My contract called for $2400 the first year.

Fitting perfectly into the landscape, Enola School was perched on a little knoll about three or four blocks from the center of town. The main building had a central meeting area that served as an auditorium and sports arena surrounded by classrooms and the administration office. The elementary classrooms were on the north end and the high school classrooms were on the south end of this main building. Two separate smaller buildings housed the cafeteria and agriculture complex. Even though weathered by years of use, one could easily see that the school was the life of the community. Basketball was the passion.

My room had a coal heater at one end, and a complete row of tall windows that could be raised or lowered on the west side. These usually supplied more than ample solar heating in summer and were a source of cold air leaks in winter. A number of electric light bulbs spaced at four to six feet intervals dangled jauntily from the ceiling. Like most rural schools at that time, air conditioning was an unaffordable luxury. The rural atmosphere had kept life simple and the students seemed happy with the status quo. One unusual tradition they observed was the split term. School was in session in the summer, out in the fall for harvesting cotton and other crops, and then reconvened to finish the school year in the spring.

Mr. and Mrs. Johnny Jobe rented an old farm house to me and I scraped together a few household necessities to "make do". The plan was for you and me to stay in Enola during the week while I was teaching, then go to Jacksonville to be with John on the week-end. Mrs. Jobe kept her little grandson, Kim Leach, who was about your age and agreed to keep you for me during the day. You two boys were real buddies. Mr. Jobe would ride you around in his pick-up truck giving you the usual boy adventures of discovery. Mrs. Jobe (Buelah) was the piano player at church. She taught you boys to sing Christian songs. You boys liked *Bringing in the Sheaves* and rendered it with much gusto and fanfare. It came out more like "bringing in the sheep" as neither of you had any idea what sheaves were.

I joined the Baptist church where the Jobes attended and enjoyed getting to know the people. John had been transferred to a road job at Leola making it not feasible to join him every week-end. On the Sundays we didn't go to see him, we went to church. I soon found out that people had so much respect for school teachers that some thought educators were well versed in all subjects including the Bible. Although my Bible knowledge was limited in many respects, I had read the entire book a couple of times by then. Soon I was asked to be the teacher for the young couples's class. I agreed thinking we would learn together. One Sunday I mentioned that Jesus had pre-existed with God and helped with the creation before he came to earth to be born as a man. Immediately an outspoken member challenged my statement implying it was heresy. I did not argue the point, but suggested that we both read the Bible for evidence for and against the statement. Frankly, I was sure it was true, but could not produce scriptures to prove it on the spur of the moment. Also, it was not my intent to argue but to learn.

I spent the whole afternoon pouring over the scriptures until I found my references. Meanwhile, the man asked the pastor who confirmed what I had said. I realized at that point, however, that I was not ready to take on deep theological discussions. My faith had been simple and perhaps too assuming. The incident did whet my appetite to learn more, and I promised myself to continue to study as much as I could.

Mrs. Jobe was an expert seamstress as was her daughter Dodie Leach who taught home economics at Mount Vernon school. Buelah stitched three lovely dresses for me to wear to school; I made one dress myself in a school sewing workshop under Buelah's direction. This time around I did not neglect to preshrink my fabric. My project turned out pretty well even though I made a poor choice of large checkered bright colored fabric which caused me to have to use an excess of material in order to match the pattern. Not used to having so many nice changes and receiving so many compliments, I felt like a princess. It gave me more self-confidence which I needed badly.

School went well. I couldn't believe I would actually get paid for doing something I enjoyed so much. It was conducted somewhat like the Palestine School I had attended as a child, but was more sophisticated in that it had electricity, indoor bathrooms, and a much larger teaching staff. I taught seventh grade geography, never thinking I might some day get to visit many of the places we talked about. The dream was still alive though. My other classes included all the high school English, a history class, and a study hall. I never liked to keep study hall, but it was good discipline for me to keep still as well as trying to get the students to do so. I remembered a story I had once read about training a horse. The father in the story told his son that he couldn't control his horse until he learned to control himself. I figured that went for students as well because I was quite the greenhorn. As sponsor of the junior and senior classes, I went on a trip with the students to Petit Jean Mountain where they swam and went boating and bicycle riding. They were curious about the little grave where legend says Petit Jean was buried. Hers was a romantic love story about a girl stowing away on a ship coming to America to be with her true love. Tragically, she died and was buried on the mountain.

After an eventful year, spring arrived, and we had a closing school ceremony similar to the one at Palestine School when I was a child. A western theme encouraged a lot of good-natured horseplay behind the scenes, but the students spurred through practice and gave a rousing jingling, jangling performance on the night of presentation to parents and friends.

I learned to love the people and students at Enola and was grateful to get a chance to launch my teaching career there, but I longed to get back closer to home. I graduated from UCA in the spring of 1963 with a BA degree in English and Social Studies. With two years of teaching behind me and a degree, I could get a better salary. John meantime had become very sick, and after having been diagnosed with emphysema, had to retire from the road job. Mr. John McCracken offered him a job in his shop at Conway, but John only worked a few days when the welding fumes landed him back in the hospital.

We struggled along on my salary of $2600 until school was out. I applied for work at several schools, finally getting a job at Grapevine School which was not too far from Sheridan. By this time, you were four years old. John could save a babysitting fee by keeping you at home while I worked. You two guys had a great time with your hunting dogs. John took you squirrel hunting. You had a gun shy dog named Snuffles that would follow you into the woods, but as soon as a shot was fired, Snuffles made a beeline back to the house. He got to the point where he would not follow along if he saw the gun. John outsmarted him by hiding the gun in his coat sleeve. He took a leash to tie Snuffles up before the gun was fired. Snuffles suffered the terror of the furies, but became a super squirrel dog.

At Christmas that winter, a seventeen inch snow fell. With a fireplace and plenty of wood, we holed up. The school coach G.E.Montgomery, his wife, and their three children came over almost every day. We all ate popcorn, drank hot chocolate, and played games. You shared your toys including a cowboy and Indian set that must have had a thousand pieces. There were outlaws, robbers, sheriffs, and Indians among the personages. Included also were fake mountains, stagecoaches, saloons, hotels, horses, and a menagerie of other assorted animals and things. Luckily we had a spare room for setup, but that set was a mother's nightmare when it came to putting it away.

With his magnetic personality and gentle nature, John got acquainted with everyone for miles around. Every neighbor had some piece of equipment for him to "look at when he felt like it." Once, the school superintendent, Bobby Daniels, asked John if he would help him fix the well pump at the black school a few miles away. John took you along. You heard kids inside the school and peeped around to see where they were. You had never seen many black people before and wanted to get a good look. The kids in turn waved and smiled at you. When recess came a few minutes later, they poured out the door and you ran over to play with them. John got the pump fixed and you two left as the bell rang and recess was over. You wanted to go back the next day and play with them some more.

Not long after we moved to Grapevine, I spotted a church near where we lived. It was Bethany No. 2 down in The Bend. I started taking you to church again. John did not feel comfortable at a new church and did not go with us, but we went anyway. One of the best things I remember about that church is a lady named Dolly Moltz that sang beautifully. Her messages in song were so moving. I also met a Taylor family who had a pretty young girl named Judy. She later married our nephew Gene Cullins who came to live with us during his junior year.

That summer I went back to UCA with you and John in tow. We left our house in Grapevine unattended and rented an apartment near the college so that I could work on my Masters Degree. One day, I bought some plastic numbers to use to teach you your numbers from zero to nine. We tried only a few at a time, but you would get them all mixed up and become frustrated. When we started home for the weekend, you were muttering as you filled your little tote bag with things to take home. I looked inside, and there were the numbers. At first I was encouraged by your initiative because I thought you intended to practice them at home. Not so! My bubble burst when I asked you why you were taking them. You said you were going to let Snuffles eat them. In your own way, you had figured out a solution to a "serious" problem.

Being a very gregarious child, you wanted someone to play with. By the time you were five you began asking for a little brother. We told you that a little brother cost a lot of money, but if you would save your money, we would see what we could find. You forego a lot of treats and special things to put every bit of money you could get into your piggy bank until it was full. The pressure was on to find that brother. Sure enough, in September of 1964, I again became pregnant. I resigned my job at the end of the fall semester because, back then, it was not common for an expectant mother to be teaching. I did agree, however, to help with junior and senior plays in evening practice. I always enjoyed drama and helping with the plays was a delight. Sound effects were especially fun. In one of the plays the scene was to be a haunted house during a rainstorm. The students designed cobwebs for the corners of the stage area, and they reflected the dim light in an eerie fashion. We hung a sheet of tin and popped it backstage to sound exactly like thunder. Stagehands flashed lights on and off to simulate lightning. Some dried peas rattling in a matchbox in front of a backstage microphone created the sound of rain. We were so good, we almost felt ourselves getting drenched! A little imagination sufficed for modern technological equipment. After one of the night performances, many people in the audience were surprised to see a clear sky outside.

The matinee performance of each drama was presented during the day for the school children. On the day of performance, some of the seniors decided that I just must be there to see them. They got permission to leave school to drive over to pick me up. On the way over they saw a wounded deer with its head hung in a fence. It was deer season and it probably was confused by hunters. The boys stopped, jumped out, and one of them finished killing it. They arrived at my house with the deer in the trunk of their car. They were exuberant but scared of getting into trouble with the game authorities. I told them to put it in my shed and close the door until I could contact the superintendent. We talked to the superintendent who in turned contacted the game warden. They agreed to let the kids have the deer to serve in the school lunchroom if they did not charge for it. The venison was served as a special side dish to the regular lunch menu. Because we had just recently finished James Fennimore Cooper's *Deerslayer* in English class, Eddie Plunkett, who killed the deer, got the honorary title of Deerslayer for the remainder of the term.

It was during my teaching career at Grapevine that a devastating historical event occurred. One morning as we were having class, word came that President John F. Kennedy had been shot in Dallas, Texas. The whole school went into mourning. He was such a beloved President. Efforts to save him were fruitless. One of my most vivid memories is the picture on television of John, Jr. saluting his father's grave as his Dad was put to rest in Arlington Cemetery. Vice President Lyndon Johnson was quickly sworn into office. That event, though tragic, proved to be a good illustration to use in teaching the stability of our democracy. Our government is structured in such a way that, if a leader is lost, another is already in line to take his place and carry on the country's business in smooth transition. I decided that as flawed as our system is in some ways, it is the best system of government in the world.

On a more personal level, my sister, Martha, died at just 42 years of age after an extended illness of several months. Lizzie and her children had moved in with Martha's family to help take care of her. This was a good arrangement for everyone because Lizzie's husband had become mentally incapacitated and was sent to Fort Roots Hospital in North Little Rock for treatment. She would not have to remain in her home way out in the woods alone with the children After Martha's death, Lizzie bought a house close to the elementary school in Sheridan in order to be closer to shopping areas and school. Lizzie had a difficult time trying to raise her four children alone, and later, she, too, had to enter a mental hospital. The children became wards of the state and were placed in foster homes. I wanted so desperately to take them, but with trying to care for my dad, you, and John and work full time, there seemed no way. I felt that they would receive better care if placed with a loving foster family. It was hard for me to realize my own limitations and not to try to do more than I could reasonably do. My heart bled to help them.

Life at Grapevine for me included a myriad of classes in English, American history, and algebra. One of my students, Betty Carey, helped me publish a newsletter that we called *The Black Cat* from the school team mascot. Basketball was the exclusive sport and created great spirit and excitement for both students and parents. Teachers took turns working the concession stand at home games.

John made friends so quickly that he soon knew more people in Grapevine than I did. One of his best friends was a logger named Cletis Taylor, with whom he swapped yarns about the logging industry and sawmilling. Cletis and his wife bought the Reynolds grocery store in Grapevine, and operated it for many years. Sid and Vernia Reed were other neighbors who lived in the "Lazy Bend". They had a number of children who were in my classes. Sid and Vernia helped John with chores and projects that were too much for him to handle by himself. Mrs. Elouise Lybrand became my hairdresser and kept me looking presentable. I loved her and her family of rowdy boys. Everyone in Grapevine was special in their own way, and I have lots of pleasant memories of the two years that I taught there.

CHAPTER 18

Teaching at Sheridan High School

In the spring of 1965, I got an offer for a job from the Sheridan School District. They needed a ninth-grade English teacher. I was delighted. I would get to go back and teach in Sheridan High School with some of the wonderful teachers that had helped me along when I was a student there. Mrs. Thornton, Mrs. Calloway, and Mr. Zimmerman among others, were still there. I was finishing up my Masters Degree that summer, and Grapevine did not have a salary scale for Master teachers at that time. It was with very mixed feelings that I left Grapevine. I had been treated royally by the students, parents, and administration, but I wanted to prove myself as a worthy teacher in my former high school. I knew there would be raised eyebrows when a person of my background began teaching there. After all, some wondered "what good thing could come out of Belfast."(Actually a lot of good things did!)

Just before my second child was born, we moved to Crossroads Community and settled in an old store building that had been renovated into an apartment. We called it the Green House because the owner had painted it a light green. My second child was born May 31, 1965. You had the privilege of naming him since Bill was on "special order". Because you loved the Wild Bill pony rider on television, you thought "Bill" would be a great name. When I finally told you I was going to the hospital to get the little brother, you were jumping for joy. You had visions of someone big enough to roughhouse with. A few days later, you were about ready to trade him back in. The "brother" had very little hair, no teeth, and could not talk or play. What a raw deal! (I had hidden your coin collection so you would think the baby had cost a lot of money.) A few days later, Mr. Clarence Barnes, owner of the store across the road, asked you what you thought of the new brother. Because you didn't want to be unkind, you answered,"I can say just one thing. He sure is 'spensible'."(Meaning expensive)

You started to school the year Bill was born. You were allowed to go to Head Start Kindergarten during that summer. John was able to drive the group of kids from Crossroads to Sheridan for the classes. What a lively bunch of kids! One little girl talked non-stop all the way there and back. Our little car seemed to be puffing in and out as it moved down the road with songs and laughter echoing from the children.

With school going well, I cast about again for a place to go to church. I felt that we all needed spiritual training. New Hope Methodist Church was diagonally across Highway 167 from our house. I started going to church there because it was convenient, I loved the people, and I had hoped that John would start going to church with me again. He claimed he was embarrassed because he couldn't read. You boys and I went together. No one seemed to mind my Baptist background. There at New Hope Church, we met Gene and Florence Plunkett. Mrs. Plunkett worked in the school lunchroom. She made the biggest, fluffiest, and most delicious rolls I had ever eaten. This couple was always doing nice things for us. Also there was Doc and Winnie Reaves. Doc had been county judge some years before. They had lost their only son in an accident. Partly to compensate for their loss, and to reach out to others, they took in foster children. One of the foster children was a girl named Linda.

Linda was a pretty teen-age girl and you boys both had a crush on her. She taught your Sunday School Class and helped me with a Christmas play. The play was called *Caves of the Earth*. It was a modern day rendition of Noah's Ark. The main characters were trying to gather up animals of every species and put them in a cave before an expected holocaust would happen. We printed out programs and practiced with all the kids in the church. Bill was a rabbit that would not stay in the cave. He was only a little over two years old, but played his part well.

To show my appreciation for her help, I bought a musical jewelry box for Linda for Christmas. It was a bright pink and had little drawers that could be pulled out to store rings and small jewelry. Bill saw the little box and wanted to play with it. I let him play with it a few minutes but then told him we had to wrap it for Linda. He became possessive and said, "No, I am not giving Linda my drawers!" I told him that was for a girl, and that I would buy him a tackle box to go fishing. He liked that idea better and relinquished the jewelry box.

We were tired of moving from place to place and wanted to settle near Sheridan close to family and friends. Mr. H.C. Gentry had two acres for sale on State Highway 35 South of Sheridan in Crossroads Community. The land had been sold to some other people who did not keep up their mortgage payments. They claimed that they were being harassed by ghosts-like beings that frequented their mobile home in the wee hours of the morning and threatened them. The sheriff investigated but could find no evidence to support their allegations. Some thought their story was made up in an attempt to recover the money they had paid down on the property. After Mr. Gentry foreclosed the property, John and I contracted to buy it. It was covered with tree stumps and brambles. John used that for his project. On days when he felt like working a little, he would go there with Bill and they would cut and burn brush. He hired a man with a road grader to level off a place for a house, but the grader got stuck. It was summer and quite dry, so we decided that spot might not be the best place to build a house. John was not to be daunted, however. He had 50 dump truck loads of gravel spread on the place. After that settled, we had a firm place to build a house.

We paid off the land mortgage in a short time, and decided to try to get a home loan using our land as collateral. John talked to the FHA agent about a low-interest home loan and got approval for enough to build a modest brick house and drill a well. We were excited at the prospect of actually owning our own home. No more cleaning filthy roach-infested apartments with greasy stoves and leaky faucets. The house was to be all electric. We opted for a fireplace because the electricity often went off for hours after an ice or wind storm. The fireplace would serve as backup heat. That idea proved not so good, though, because it sucked the heat up the chimney instead of warming the house as we thought. We later blocked it off and put a wood heater in front of it. Our little bungalow consisted of two small bedrooms, a tiny bath, kitchen, living room, utility room, and car port. By today's standards, that would be a small house for four people, but we considered it a castle.

School was great. You and I rode back and forth together, and John took care of Bill. When we came home from school, John would often be driving the tractor in the garden, and Bill would be asleep on his shoulder. We all helped dig a septic tank hole with trenches for field lines and had a tank put down. It was great fun to watch our place being transformed.

John managed to get some antique wagon wheels and cemented them on each side of the driveway culvert thus giving the place a bit of western flavor. You always watched his every move as he worked and later described the scene in a story you wrote about your memories of him. You said that John had used the wagon wheels in an object lesson for you. John explained that the spokes in the wheel were the same length making the wheel work perfectly. He said if one spoke had been shorter or longer, the wheel would not work. Then he used that to represent people. Some think of themselves as "bigger" or "better" or more important than others. That causes relationships to not work well. He explained that God loves all people and wants them to pull together like the spokes in the wagon wheel. If we do that as our family is doing, there is nothing we can not do together. Your dad drew wisdom from proverbs and wise sayings and always seemed to have just the right one handy at the right time.

You said that you mused over what John had said as your dad put a few finishing touches on his labor. Then, picking up the tools, John asked, "Want a ride?" You scrambled upon the broad shoulders of his back and smiled as though you were on top of the world as you two moved toward the house. You said you remembered thinking, "I want to be like the wagon wheel."

You remember how John loved to fish. He bought a flat-bottomed boat, fishing gear, and a boat motor and took us all fishing as often as he could. We made lots of trips to Cox Creek at Leola and sometimes to Lake Conway, Harris Brake Lake, and the Lakes around Hot Springs I can't remember ever catching many fish, but we had fun just being out in the open air and seeing nature at its best. Another family activity we enjoyed was beekeeping. At one time we had about 35 hives of bees that supplied us with plenty of honey and pollinated our garden. We all had bee hats and white coveralls to help rob the bees. John rarely got stung even though he often wore only a t-shirt top when he worked with them.

I was not quite so lucky. One day while I was mowing the grass near the beehives, the smoke and noise from the mower caused the bees to be upset. They swarmed out at me and filled my hair full of bees. I panicked and started slapping at them. That just made matters worse. They kept stinging and stinging me on the head. I bent my head to the ground and moaned not knowing what to do. Then it suddenly came to me to drown them. I rushed to the house and poured water all over my head. I was home alone and did not know how I would get the stingers out. One of Bill's teenage friends came by to see him, and picked the stingers out for me. We counted seventy-five stingers. I could feel my tissues swelling against my brain, and should have gone to a doctor immediately, but just toughed it out. It took a week or two for me to feel normal again. I blamed myself for not realizing I would provoke the bees with the noise and smoke, but that was certainly another lesson learned.

Somehow in all the interactions of family activities, Bill got the idea that he belonged to John, and you belonged to me. To Bill, everybody was some kind of Momma (except me). He called John "Momma", a neighbor that raised chickens was "Chicken Momma," her neighbor who was heavy set was "Big Mamma", and the mail carrier lady was "Mail Momma." (I felt a little left out) That was not really a problem for a time because everybody had somebody, but when John grew deathly ill in 1970, I realized that Bill was afraid his dad would die, and he would not have anybody. I had to reassure him that I was his mother and that I loved him the same as I did you. Bill began first grade that year, and his teacher, Mrs. Leona Buck, rode the school bus from the elementary school to the high school with him for the first few days so he would feel more secure. I was ever so grateful for her kindness.

John gradually got better and came home, but the emphysema progressed slowly, making it hard for him to breathe. Some of the medicines, especially phenergan, made him hallucinate. He had to go for a stay in the hospital three or four times a year. He was changing in so many ways, and I didn't know what to do to help him. He became paranoid, thinking people were out to get us, listening in on every conversation, following us everywhere we went, and growing marijuana in the woods around our house. I tried to convince him that we were not important enough for people to care what we said; that no one was going to hurt us. He would not walk around the house into the woods with me so I could show him nothing strange was growing there.

I struggled with myself trying to understand and help him at the same time. Deep inside I knew it was a losing battle that we had to fight together no matter the cost. You boys were frustrated because your Dad did not want you to go outside and play. You could only stand so much television. I thought of my Dad and what he had endured with Mom. History was repeating itself in the pattern of my life except now I was in the driver's seat and didn't know exactly where I was going. I tried to keep your lives as normal as possible, and we invited all the kids in our neighborhood to come and play as they always had. Your cousin, Jimbo, would spend time with us when his mom was working and I was not in school. Remember how Jimbo would delight us by singing "Raindrops Falling on My Head?"

John was on more and more medications as his condition progressed. The doctor ordered oxygen and a hospital bed at our home. Breathing became increasing difficult as the sound of wheezing and coughing constantly reminded me that John was dying a slow, painful death. He would squat on his legs and cough a coffee can full of amber mucus every night. One night he begged me to rub his back harder and harder as he groaned with intense pain. I felt he might not live until morning. Dr. Irvin came down to our house about 2 a.m. He gave John an injection for the pain and albuterol puffs to make it easier for him to breathe. Gradually he relaxed and fell asleep.

The next morning he slid off his hospital bed and crawled to the bathroom for a smoke. A wave of such pity washed over me. I marveled that the cigarettes that helped to cause his suffering were so addictive and would bring a strong man to his knees. That morning, his head seemed to be clearer for rational thought than it had been for some time. He told me he wanted to go to the State Hospital for treatment. Remembering my mother's tragedy, I shuddered at the thought and went on to school trying to dismiss it from my mind and to come up with a better alternative.

As soon as I left, John called his sister, June, who then worked at the State Hospital Cafeteria in the Benton Unit. He begged her to come down and help him get committed. She hurried down from Benton to see about him. As always, June tried to do anything she could for John, but she felt that this was a little much. She came up to the high school and called me out to talk. We both cried, then decided we would take him to Dr. Irvin's office to see what could be worked out. It was so comforting to have June to share this problem with me as I had run out of ideas and was almost a basket case myself. Dr. Irvin took us in right away. He was opposed to sending John to the State Hospital, but John insisted, and the doctor finally gave in.

What a God-send that was after all! Dr. Thomas Burford, a psychiatrist, took his case. It was baffling to everyone. I left John there for a few days observation. When I went back to see him, his regular clothes had been removed, and he was dressed in rags. His scrawny frame looked gaunt and emaciated. Long arms and legs were sticking out of the shirt sleeves and pants legs; his hair was disheveled, and shoe strings were flopping.

There was strangeness about him. It was as though he had found refuge behind the bars and no longer felt threatened by the imaginary evils he had feared. I thanked God for the progress made in medications from the time my mother was treated. John stayed three months and then came home with a sack full of medications to keep him stabilized. Despite his suffering, John was neither violent nor unreasonably grumpy. It would have been difficult to care for him indeed if he had turned against me as my mother sometimes had done my dad.

When I almost despaired, I thought of Dad. How had he cared for five children and worked to feed them? My life had turned full circle, back to the same problem that confused me as a child. Now, I felt the full force of the fury as an adult. I still had only questions with no answers. To compensate, I buried myself in my teaching and tried to raise you and Bill as best I could. I did a lot of praying, too, and that seemed to calm me between the storms. I remembered a story entitled "Footprints in the Sand" where Jesus carried the person when he was too weak to travel on his own. I hoped that he would carry me just a little way. Many times I felt a sense of loss, and loneliness would overtake me. Quiet tears would come to relieve me for the moment until I could get my bearings again. Like Job, I pleaded with God to let me know the reason why. I wanted to call a heavenly tribunal to declare that I had done nothing to deserve all this. Then I would remember the innocent one that took the sins of the whole world on Himself because of His love for an ungrateful people. Maybe I would understand better in time to come. I would muddle through this trial hoping for strength to endure.

Once, you boys and I started to the hospital to see John. We got about 10 miles up the Benton Highway, and the complete motor fell out of the car. I got a wrecker to tow us back home. The wrecker attendant looked under the car and saw that the bolts had come out of the motor mount. He jacked the motor back under the car and replaced the bolts in the mounts, and we were ready to go again.

The next day, we tried again. We got to the hospital for our visit. I had stopped at a burger place and got you boys burgers and fries to eat. You were too young to be allowed inside the hospital, so I found a shady place to park and cautioned you to stay in the car with the doors locked. You ate what you could of your meals then noticed a flock of pigeons on the ground near the car. You decided to roll the window down just enough to throw the scraps to the pigeons. Just as you did that, you saw a man stealthily approaching the car. You hurriedly rolled the window back up and slunk down in the seat terrified but daring to look again and again to see if he was still coming. The man kept coming, but bent down lower to the ground as though trying to hide behind the car. Suddenly, in one fell swoop, he scooped up a half-eaten burger and hurried off eating it. The pigeons fluttered then settled back. You recovered quickly from the surprise and started laughing.

After a few more visits, you boys got a little braver because you realized that the patients that had ground privileges were not violent. One afternoon before we left the hospital grounds, you wanted to go to the patient canteen just around the corner. I gave you guarded permission but sat in the car keeping a close watch on you. A man stepped out in front of you, extended his hand, and said, "Hi, I'm George! (not the real name). You took the extended hand for a quick handshake, but the man gripped your hand and shook and shook for some time. I could see your face turning red and knew you were wondering how to get away. Just as quickly the man released your hand and hurried along.

We laughed and sang together, and I tried to put up a brave front, but many times I almost despaired. At length I found a poster that inspired me. Strange, how little things can make a big difference. The poster had a lemon squeezer on it. It said, "When life gives you lemons, make lemonade." I decided that was what I would try to do.

For you boys, I worked hard at being the best mother I could be, and have always been grateful for your forgiveness when I fell short. (I never could find the instruction booklet that came with you)

For my students and co-workers, I worked hard at being the best teacher I could be. In the 1970's, the Sheridan Jaycees honored me by naming me "Teacher of the Year." Even though, I didn't feel I was the most outstanding teacher in the system, I felt honored to represent more than 100 great teachers with whom I worked.

My family joined Calvary Missionary Baptist Church in the early 1970's. You boys seemed happy to have a church family that gave us love and support. I taught Sunday School classes and helped with Bible School. I wanted you children to have the spiritual comfort of knowing Christ as personally as I know him and seeing what a difference God's Love can make in the life of a believer.

Somehow, we managed to get through the years it took for you boys to grow up. You married at sixteen to a lovely girl who was seventeen. You were both so young that the marriage was turbulent and lasted only two years. Later you met and married Nell Stage who became the mother of my two grandsons, David and Brian. When that marriage seemed to not be working out, you joined the navy .You both tried an on-again off-again relationship until that marriage also ended in divorce. Nell returned with the boys to Little Rock to be near her family. After you got out of the navy you lived in the mobile home here at Belfast. Since you had been a Corpsman in the navy, you worked as a ward clerk at Saline County Hospital until you could challenge the LPN test to become a licensed nurse. Nell was good about letting our family keep the boys as often as we liked on week-ends and their school vacations. It became routine for me to head to Little Rock to pick up the boys as soon as school was out on Friday afternoons.

To share expenses, you had a roommate, J. P. Ward, whom we all liked. You and J.P. would take Brian and David to DeGray Lake for an outing as often as you could. You would all swim, gather shells, and build sandcastles. The boys loved to ride in the back of the Toyota pickup and hang on for dear life around the curves of the back roads you drove.After one typical outing, you returned in the late evening and the boys burst through my kitchen door to tell me about the day's happenings.

"Granny, you shoulda seen our sandcastle!" David exclaimed, his eyes sparkling, red sunburned face shining, swim jacket and flip flops dangling and his beach towel dragging.

"Yeah!" Brian piped up, pushing his way ahead of David while getting his towel untangled from the door. "It was big and high…and…uh…" He groped for words in his three-year-old vocabulary but could not find the suitable adjectives. I understood clearly, however, because his chubby little arms were expanded full length and his eyes were full of suppressed excitement.

David, who was five, pushed past Brian pressuring him authoritatively aside, and continued his account of the sand castle they had built at the beach on Lake DeGray that Sunday afternoon. "P.J. (They always mixed up J.P.'s initials.) and Daddy helped us make it. We piled up a big heap of sand," he added, making an outline and patting motions with his hands. "And then we made a ditch around it like this (more gestures) and some really high walls. We put water in the ditch, too."

"Moat," J.P. corrected. Up to now he had stood behind the boys, himself beaming with excitement and trying to restrain the urge to help them tell their story. "Remember, castles have a moat. That is a special kind of ditch. And what did we put in the moat?" he prompted.

"A alligator," both responded at the same time. "Only it was really just some little sticks," David confided. "We don't want no real alligators. No siree."

"And how did the people cross the moat?" asked J.P.

"Oh, yeah, we built a drawbridge. In old days the people could cross on the drawbridge. Then they pulled it up behind them like Grandpa's tractor lift. Sometimes bad men chased them to the castle, and they runned across the bridge," David informed me. I thought what a great object lesson laced with medieval history.

"And...and...the bad men slid right off into the alligator moat when the bridge popped up." Brian added.

At this point David and Brian busied themselves with a pantomime of actions depicting imaginary, noisy battle scenes at the castle. You hurried them off to the bathroom to clean themselves up. In the brief calm, J.P. dropped into a nearby chair while I handed him a glass of iced tea. He accepted it gratefully. He then began his own account of the sandcastle, and I was anxious for more details. "We did have a lot of fun," he admitted, "and we made the whole thing with just a few rocks, some mussel shells, seaweed, and sand. No one paid any attention at first, but some people standing by soon seem to think it was funny to see two grown men on their knees in the sand helping to build a sandcastle. Before long, this paunchy man of about fifty casually drifted over to get a better look. He was probably a business man used to the inside because he squinted in spite of his sun visor, and his legs were white and downy sticking out of those Bermuda shorts.

After he stood there watching a few minutes, he got around to saying, "Whatcha doing?"

We simply answered, "Building a sandcastle."

He laughed and said, "Well, I'll be damned!" We made small talk for a bit, mostly talking about the sandcastle. He decided the little ones needed some mussel shells to put on the castle. The boys thought that a good idea and went with him along the water's edge and found some nice shells. On the way back, Brian was distracted by a crawfish. He picked it up gingerly by the back and brought it back wiggling and squirming.

By this time, Claud and I were really into this thing. We wanted this sandcastle to be impressive. Three young boys started watching us. They kept edging closer like they wanted to help, but didn't want to ask. Finally, I asked them if they knew how to build a moat. I said I sure could use some help with that. They quickly transformed into animated bulldozers. Some girls nearby giggled and dug their toes in the sand. 'Look at what cool designs you can make with your feet,' they offered.

Claud had shrugged and said, "What the heck?" I nodded and told them they could imprint some designs on the walls if they wanted. You'd think they had won the Little Miss DeGray pageant.

Everyone was so intent that we didn't see the two ladies come up. One was the wife of the man in the Bermuda shorts. She pulled her sunglasses down on her nose and looked like she couldn't believe her eyes. "Fred," she joked to him, "I might have known you'd be acting like a kid." Fred paid no attention to her.

A little boy about three waddled up with a sand bucket. He didn't hang back like the older kids had done, but just got up for a good close look. He then reached into his pail and produced a frog which he placed very decisively in front of the castle door. Everyone laughed and said that was a fine frog, and someone suggested that It probably was bewitched and would someday turn into a handsome prince. Brian and David looked at the little boy and decided he would make a good friend, so they asked him to help them find some more shells. They soon gathered half a bucket of shells which the girls placed on the castle. Some other people brought colorful rocks to put on the wall for a masonry look. By this time, everyone on the beach was enthralled by the castle. We all stood back to take a look. Someone suggested it needed a flag. Some seaweed woven on a stick just fixed it right up. I really think that is the largest and finest sandcastle ever built on Lake DeGray," J. P. concluded.

You came back in as J.P. finished the tale, and said, "Not just the biggest on Lake DeGray, but the biggest in Arkansas. And I got pictures, Mom. We'll show you."

We were jarred back to the present as the noise from the bathroom reached a crescendo. You rushed back to conduct dressing rituals. Brian and David dried off, put on pajamas, and after mild protests, went dutifully off to bed. You followed to make sure they settled in. Brian gave you a big hug and said simply and honestly, "I like sandcastles."

"I do, too," David agreed. "They help you make friends."

As you turned out the light and started back to the kitchen, I could hear David ask one last question, "Daddy, how long will our sandcastle be there?"

"Well...I really don't know. It looks like rain tonight." You answered quietly.

"I know," I thought to myself. "That sandcastle will be there as long as there are two little boys that had a fun day at the beach with their daddy. It will be there as long as anyone remembers and takes pleasure in thinking about what it was like today. Neither rain, nor wind, nor time can erase the joy that is in the heart."

That was just one of many times we made good memories. Bill would take Brian and David fishing and camping, and mule riding. I would let them help me in the garden. They made a goat cart and helped with the chickens. I bought a camcorder and took videos of some of their fun activities.

As time passed, Bill was President of his local 4-H Club and was chief bench warmer on the Stinger Football Team. He began raising Duroc hogs as an Agriculture project at school and for the 4H Club. He won blue ribbons at the Grant County,

Regional, and State Fairs for his prize Durocs. As a junior in High School, he got on the GCE program and worked at the Sheridan Hardware Store for the Balwanz family. He saved his money and bought his own truck including the insurance. He was naïve and restless, however, and soon tore out the transmission with mud riding and track racing. As a result of his interest in auto mechanics class in high school, he chose to specialize in transmission work after he graduated. He went to transmission school for a short time, worked for AAMCO, and then for Razorback Transmissions on Geyer Springs in Little Rock. All the while he dreamed of having his very own shop. With a little financial help from us, he built a 50 by 50 ft. shop. We loved having him work here at home, and John liked the hustle and bustle of people always coming in and out. (I did, too, except for the grease they tracked into my house.) Bill continued to work at Razorback Transmissions and fix transmissions in his shop on nights and weekends.

It seemed my life was always about family. No matter what happened that either surprised or pleased me in a good way or disappointed me in other ways, I always felt inseparably linked to all of them. I had no logical explanation. That is just the way it was. Time passed and you and Bill found your own separate niches in life. David and Brian grew to manhood and gradually found their own ways of choice.

John and I were mostly alone to adapt to an empty nest. John's breathing continued to get more laborious. He could be heard wheezing and coughing constantly. At one point he broke a rib from coughing so hard. He was on oxygen and seldom got outside the house. The difference in the temperature, humidity, and barometric pressure affected him. The doctors increased and/or changed his medicines frequently to help him get more quality from life.

In 1984, I became ill. My head hurt constantly; the left side of my face was numb; my throat felt constricted and talking was difficult. Then came the noises in my left ear. I had never heard of tinnitus, but now I was very much aware of it. "What was happening to me?' I wondered. Teaching became a struggle because even the noise of the air conditioner made the head noises worse. I went to Dr. Kyser, an ENT, who prescribed a two-week round of prednisone. He thought I might have fluid in the inner ear as a result of some flu-like symptoms I had had earlier. The medicine did not help.

I went to three other specialists, each giving a different diagnosis, but none had any real help. I had lost 90% hearing in the left ear. For four years, I tried different types of hearing aids and medications. By this time, my nerves were shot. I would be so tense during the day trying to ignore the tinnitus and focus on my teaching that when I tried to relax at night, tears would flow unabashed despite all efforts to keep them within. I felt near to madness. What could I do? If I quit teaching, I would have no health insurance. If I didn't, I thought I might break down completely and be no good to myself or others. Who would take care of John? I checked into my teacher retirement program. After I gathered my medical reports and sent an application, I was accepted as disabled. One catch was that I would have to pay the full amount of health insurance out of my retirement check since the school would no longer match the health premiums for an inactive teacher. That alone took $500 per month, half of my retirement check.

CHAPTER 19

Decisions and Adjustments

I had to do something! Retirement was blessed! No matter that we had so little money to meet our bills. I just stayed at home for a while and enjoyed working in my garden, doing a few crafts, taking care of John, and pulling my thoughts together. John had to have help with bathing now and getting him in and out of the tub was a major chore. He had gained weight until he was almost 300 pounds. He understood so little about dieting that when I attempted to help him limit his intake, he tried to cooperate at mealtime but would raid the refrigerator for snacks between times and sometimes eat a half jar of mayonnaise. To add to the almost unbearable difficulty of John's health problems, his sister, June died in the late 1980's followed in a short time by my dad.

I became almost despondent at times and tried hard to keep my spirits up as best I could. I have always found that when life seems difficult, I need to look around and try to help others. There is always someone worse off. The local Laubach Literacy Program under the direction of a retired teacher friend, Mary Harper gave me the chance. I tutored a few students there and volunteered a few hours a week at SOS, a local organization that supplied services for the poor. Sandra Wallace, the overall director of GCUCRC, asked me to be the TEA coordinator for Grant County. She allowed me to work part time as I could arrange it. It was good therapy for me to get out among people as much as I could, but soon John was very ill again and was in the hospital. The ladies there were so supportive and understanding of my situation, that I really regretted having to leave.

After that, I stayed home most of the time trying to occupy myself with activities. My tinnitus problem had gradually improved, but I never regained the hearing in my left ear. I found out about a state law that allows senior citizens over sixty to take college courses tuition free if there is room in a class for them. I had always loved school anyway, so decided that was something I could do. I would only be gone for a few hours of class, then back home for study. I enrolled in Spanish and piano classes at UAPB. That was such fun! I studied hard but both classes made me more aware of my hearing difficulty. I finished both and received a grade of "A" for each.

After that, I tried taking private piano lessons for a while. I could not yet read the notes fast enough to get my timing right. Mostly, I just made noise which caused John to have worse headaches. He didn't complain, but I knew and felt guilty. In the fall of 1998, I enrolled in another Spanish class at SEARK College at Pine Bluff. I could play my tapes using my headphones and not be a bother to John. That worked out great! My semester at UAPB and work with the Literacy Program teaching the Spanish people at Leola was an asset in that class. I took a few other classes in computer there also.

The next spring, my Spanish teacher, Dr. Sara Hardin, was taking a group on a trip to England, Ireland, and Wales. She asked me if I would like to go. Of course, I wanted to, but my circumstances were not conducive. I talked to my friend, Odie Lewis, who traveled a lot and asked her if she would be interested. Odie did not like the idea of riding a plane, but decided she would go. You realized how desperately I needed a break and encouraged me to go. You reminded me that you were a nurse and could take care of your dad. Our grandson, Brian, was living with us at the time also, so I decided to go. I had never ridden on a plane either, but was not worried about that. It was so great to not feel like a potted plant.

The trip was wonderful and refreshed my dreams. I had never thought that I would get to see the London Bridge where the Canterbury pilgrims walked or the replica of Shakespeare's Theater where so many great Shakespeare plays are still being performed. The whole world seemed to be spread out before me for the brief nine days that we toured.

Back home again, I had my seven rolls of film processed and shared my pictures and journal notes with John and other family members. They were all glad for me that I had dared such a once-in-a-lifetime venture. And I was glad, feeling that I could do the necessary things in my life with renewed energy and better spirits.

In 2000, I was taking my fourth semester of Spanish. John was not doing well at all. His nerves were so bad that he cried almost all the time. In early March, he was hospitalized again.

I had to stay at the hospital with him. I called Dr. Hardin and told her that I would have to drop the Spanish class. She encouraged me not to drop, that I could make up the work when things calmed down. So I sat near John's bedside with my notes and tape recorder and studied while I watched over him. He died in late March, only about four months before our 50th wedding anniversary. I was happy for him because he had suffered so much, but there was an empty void in my heart that I knew not how to fill.

I went back to SEARK College after John's funeral and finished the semester. I stayed after final exam to tell Dr. Hardin goodbye and thank her so much for her wonderful friendship and understanding. That was the last Spanish class I could take at SEARK. Dr. Hardin said, "No, you are not getting off that easy. We need an English teacher here at SEARK." I was unsure if I could do that, but decided to try to teach one class that summer. I have now taught a few classes as an adjunct teacher each semester for seven years.

School was a great diversion for me. I kept making my garden every year and writing. Since 2002, I have gone on an educational tour each year with my friends at Seark. We have gone to England, France, Spain, Germany, Russia, Greece, Italy, Mexico, China, Australia, New Zealand, Peru, Hawaii, and the Fiji Islands. Those adventures are another story in themselves. I like reliving them by making presentations to groups and showing my souvenirs and photos from the tours.

Another wonderful enrichment in my recent life has been gained through connection to the internet. I can keep in touch with the friends I met and strengthen family ties with frequent email and Messenger contacts. It is so much easier to share ideas and photos in real time. Among the very special friends I have met are Lois Henson and Denise Desbians. Lois is from North Carolina, but recently moved to Virginia Beach after the death of her husband. Lois likes to write children's stories and has published a few of them. Denise is from Canada. She helped her daughter in a boutique until the daughter died of cancer and her husband of 45 years died a few months later. She is presently trying to adjust to macular degeneration that is limiting her activities. We comfort and encourage one another, and talk of brighter things.

Another special friend I met on the net is Tom Dugger from Utah who loves to travel as I do. Tom has emailed pictures of his trips to Turkey, Brazil, and the Philippines, all places which I have not yet seen. Tom is a devout Mormon, and through his sharing his faith, I have come to understand a lot about a religion that is grossly misunderstood in the area I live in. In addition to Tom, I have met Larry Gaithe from Fort Smith, a retired army nurse who had not seen his mother since he was a little boy. Eventually he found her in a nursing home in New Orleans only to have her die a short time later. Larry also lost a son to suicide but has found comfort in the companionship of his two little dogs, Tammy and Tiffany. These are just a few of the many people who have broadened my horizons and have helped me in their own way more than they can really know.

Not only does the internet provide me with a select group of special friends, but I can also search out any subject I want to know about in a few short minutes; whereas before the net, it would take days and months of researching. I can compare prices and shop right from my own home for any item I wish to purchase. I can bank online and have access to my account at any hour of the day or night. If I have a leisure moment, I can play board games either alone or with a net companion. The possibilities are endless. Surely the internet can enrich the life of anyone if they learn to use it in a way that will benefit them.

Among other recent spectacular changes in my life was my lovely new daughter-in-law, Penny. She is from England and has a charming British accent. She and her parents, Alan and Sheila, have introduced us to interesting British customs and traditions. The birth of my granddaughter, Shelby, born in September, 2001, was also the answer to my prayers. It seems that when the Lord mercifully took John, He gracefully replaced him with Shelby. Shelby lives with her parents, Bill and Michele, directly across the road from me. I love her so much. Two years later, Shelby's little sister, Mackinzee was born. What a pair they make! They are both as pure and beautiful as sunshine. Brian and Sarah have confided that they will soon make me a great grandmother to another little girl. What more could I ask? I have tried to breathe life deeply. I don't want to be afraid to try new things or miss the joy of meeting new friends.

So you can see, Claud, that my life had lowly beginnings here at Belfast. It was here that I made mistakes and learned tough lessons that helped me accept and love all the people who helped to make it so. I can still feel the love and struggles of people long since gone back to be with God to give their own accounts to Him. I have just begun to understand why we are commanded to love God with all our heart and love each other as we love ourselves. It is only through obedience to those commands that we purify our own hearts and minds from bitterness and hatred and realize peace and joy unspeakable.

CHAPTER 20

Back to the Present

Mom finished her story with a smile and a far away look in her eye. I had the feeling that her story had just paused and her life mission had not really ended. The sun was sinking lower in the west. We finished our yard work, picked up tools, and headed for our separate homes.

Bill and Claude

Lossie

Ellen

Harrington Kids

Henderson Family

John's Family Tree

Lossie's Family

About the Author

The author, Lossie Rainbolt, known by her friends as "Smiley Face," has BA and MSE degrees from UCA at Conway, AR. She likes to share the adventures of growing up in Belfast, a small, country, railroad town in central Arkansas. Schooled by hard knocks during the Depression Era, she gradually fulfilled her version of the American Dream by defying the odds, going to college and becoming a teacher. Her teaching career has spanned more than three decades. Now in her seventies, she is still teaching at SEARK College in Pine Bluff, AR, writing stories and poems, and enjoying her grandchildren. She has traveled to fourteen foreign countries in the past seven years to experience the cultures and customs. She especially likes people, enjoys family and friends and delights in hearing from former students.